To
CHRIS COTTRELL
_____

From
Pastor NATHANIEL
CARRINGTON

MEN
WOMEN
MARRIAGE

MEN
WOMEN
MARRIAGE

42 DAYS TO VICTORIOUS LIVING

My people are destroyed from lack of knowledge.

Hosea 4:6

Nathaniel Carrington

CARRICONEC PUBLICATIONS 2018

Hardcover edition
ISBN-13: 978-0-9906016-4-7
ISBN-10: 0-9906016-4-1

Men Women Marriage
42 Days to Victorious Living
Copyright © 2018 by Nathaniel B. Carrington
Book design by Carriconec

Pastor Nathaniel Carrington
P.N.B. Carrington Ministries
P.O.BOX 590584
NEWTON CENTER, MA 02459
pnbcministries.com
pastorcarrington@pnbcministries.com

All rights reserved. This book or parts thereof may not be reproduced in any form, stored in any retrieval system, or transmitted in any form by any means—electronic, mechanical, photocopy, recording, or otherwise—without prior written permission of the publisher, except as provided by United States of America copyright law. For permission, please direct your inquiries to publications@carriconec.com

Unless otherwise indicated, all scripture quotations are taken from the Holy Bible, New International Version (NIV) and the King James Version (KJV). Much of the information used in this book is based on real-world knowledge gained through my experience as a Biblical counselor. In all cases, the names and identifying information have been removed for privacy reasons.

This book has been catalogued with the Library of Congress.

DISCLAIMER: Nathaniel Carrington is a Biblical counselor, not a licensed professional counselor. Therefore, the information provided in this book is designed to provide helpful information on the subjects discussed. This book is not meant to be used, nor should it be used, to diagnose or treat any medical or psychological condition of the readers. It is sold with the understanding that the author and publisher are not engaged to render any type of psychological, legal, or any other kind of professional advice. The content of each page is the sole expression and opinion of its author, and not necessarily that of the publisher. No warranties or guarantees are expressed or implied by the publisher's choice to include any of the content in this volume. Neither the publisher nor the individual author shall be liable for any physical, psychological, emotional, financial, or commercial damages, including, but not limited to, special, incidental, consequential, or other damages. Our views and rights are the same: you are responsible for your own choices, actions, and results.

DEDICATION

This book is dedicated to the memory of my father, the late Oscar Frederick Carrington. It is also dedicated to my mother, the late Myrtle Ianthe Carrington, whose commitment to her children and her faith never wavered. And To my lovely wife, Carolyn, whose continual support, love, and patience keeps our family strong.

ACKNOWLEDGMENTS

I would like to express my most profound gratitude to the many people who made this book possible, including those whose names are not mentioned here. I recognize that I could not have completed this book without the help of the Almighty God, my loving wife Carolyn, our beautiful children, Daniel, Gabriella, and John, and close friends and relatives. I would also like to thank the many individuals who have contributed to this ministry and shared their knowledge during private and public counseling sessions and conferences throughout the years. To God be the Glory through his son Jesus Christ forever and ever Amen.

CONTENTS

PREFACE...xv

INTRODUCTION...xvii
    MARRIAGE..xviii
    SCRIPTURES xx
    THE VOW xxi
    THE JOURNEY..xxii

WEEK I: BEFORE MARRIAGE 1
    Day 1: MY HUSBAND 3
    Day 2: MY WIFE 7
    Day 3: MY IN-LAWS..11
    Day 4: MY RELIGION 15
    Day 5: MY OBLIGATIONS 19
    Day 6: MY WORK..23
    Day 7: MY MATURITY 27

WEEK II: AFTER MARRIAGE 31
    Day 8: TWO BECOME ONE............................33
    Day 9: RESPECT 37
    Day 10: SUBMISSION 41
    Day 11: SERVICE 45
    Day 12: SEX..49
    Day 13: LEADERSHIP 53

Day 14: DECISIONS 57

WEEK III: RESPONSIBILITIES 61
   Day 15: EXPECTATIONS 63
   Day 16: FINANCES 67
   Day 17: CHILDREN 71
   Day 18: FOOD 75
   Day 19: APPAREL 79
   Day 20: PRIVACY 83
   Day 21: COUNSELING 87

WEEK IV: CHALLENGES 91
   Day 22: FEAR 93
   Day 23: SUCCESS 97
   Day 24: INNOCENT UNTIL 101
   Day 25: AGE 105
   Day 26: COMPARING 109
   Day 27: CONFLICT 113
   Day 28: FRIENDSHIPS 117

WEEK V: FAILURE 121
   Day 29: FRUSTRATION 123
   Day 30: EXHAUSTION 127
   Day 31: PORNOGRAPHY 131
   Day 32: INFIDELITY 140

Day 33: FAILURE 144

Day 34: BETRAYAL 148

Day 35: DIVORCE 152

WEEK VI: GRACE 156

Day 36: FORGIVENESS 158

Day 37: TIMEOUT 162

Day 38: ISOLATION 166

Day 39: HONESTY 170

Day 40: REPENTANCE 174

Day 41: LOVE 178

Day 42: PRAYER 182

ADDITIONAL READING 186

SELF-FULFILLING PROPHECY 188

TESTIMONIALS 194

TESTIMONIAL I 195

TESTIMONIAL II 196

TESTIMONIAL III 197

TESTIMONIAL IV 198

TESTIMONIAL V 199

TESTIMONIAL VI 200

TESTIMONIAL VII 201

TESTIMONIAL VIII 202

DAILY QUOTES 204
DEVOTION NOTES 216
ABOUT THE AUTHOR 222
    PASTOR CARRINGTON 223

PREFACE

Today's men and women are inundated with many choices of books on love and marriage. Each one is waiting to be snatched off the store shelf by people from all walks of life. While the information found in these publications is usually helpful, they can never replace the time and effort needed to build a strong and vibrant marriage. Unfortunately, desperate people seeking quick answers will try anything, no matter how unlikely it is that it will provide a solution. This behavior is no different from that of a drowning man or woman grasping at a straw to save their own life.

In Men Women Marriage, Nathaniel Carrington tackles some of the hardcore issues faced by frustrated men and women, while shedding light on the core beliefs and values shared by successful people. Uncover the truths about traditional and contemporary behaviors that lead to better communication and proper decision-making. Learn how this classical approach can help individuals regain the sound judgment needed to make healthy choices.

INTRODUCTION

SUCCESSFUL MARRIAGES ARE INTENTIONAL NOT INCIDENTAL

MARRIAGE

Marriage, like many other institutions, requires that two unique individuals of opposite sexes conscientiously work together as a unit for the betterment of both. The idea that two people can coexist despite their differences continue to be one of life's greatest triumphs. Irrespective of the divorce rate and problematic relationships, getting married continues to be accepted by most cultures as one of the greatest expressions of human love. Regrettably, more and more people, especially young adults, are opting out on this union. Many of them prefer mostly to cohabit or remain bachelors and bachelorettes.

This prestigious institution, once highly desired by many, is now being shunned by some as being irrelevant and outdated. Contrary to these beliefs, it is important to note that it is the associated challenges, and not the institution, that causes these anxieties. Marriage, when approached correctly, can be very gratifying, both spiritually and naturally. The excitement of finding someone to love and be loved by is paramount to achieving most things in life. The prospect of having a bright and happy future, regardless of the unique challenges, still exists. While unforeseen difficulties and conflicts can sometimes hamper a couple's dreams or destroy their relationship, you do not have to fall prey to them.

You can still have a healthy marriage if you seek God's approach to handling life's problems (Hosea 4:6). I am not saying that adhering to specific principles will solve all marital problems. However, being knowledgeable about these challenges can prove enormously helpful when facing them (1 Peter 3:7). Therefore, the author hopes that the information found in this book will help you to do that while avoiding many of the pitfalls that lead to a failed marriage.

SCRIPTURES

Husbands, love your wives, just as Christ also loved the church and gave Himself up for her, so that He might sanctify her, having cleansed her by the washing of water with the word.

Ephesians 5:25-26

Now as the church submits to Christ, so also wives should submit to their husbands in everything.

Ephesians 5:24

Likewise, ye husbands, dwell with them according to knowledge, giving honor unto the wife, as unto the weaker vessel, and as being heirs together of the grace of life; that your prayers be not hindered.

1 Peter 3:7

My people are destroyed for lack of knowledge.

Hosea 4:6

THE VOW

It is better not to make a vow than
to make one and not fulfill it

Ecclesiastes 5:4-5

THE COMMITMENT

I, (name), take you (name), to be my (wife/husband), to
have and to hold from this day forward

THE CONTRACT

For better or for worse, for richer, for poorer, in sickness
and in health, to love and to cherish; from this day forward
until death do us part.

THE COMMAND

Be fruitful, and multiply, and replenish
the earth, and subdue it: and have dominion over the fish of
the sea, and over the fowl of the air, and over every living
thing that moveth.

Genesis 1:28

THE JOURNEY

Unlike many of the fictitious characters found in our favorite fairy tales, real couples, regardless of their circumstances, experience difficulties before and after marriage. While this may be difficult for some to understand, marital problems are not figments of spouse's imagination. Instead, they are the unpredictable challenges associated with the institution called marriage.

In contrast to the idea of a prince and princess living carefree after overcoming all odds, life after the wedding day for many couples is far less fanciful. No matter how relatable these stories may seem, building a future based on a fable is not the wisest way to start a relationship. The truth is, while some stories can convey inspirational life messages, they at times stop short of exemplifying how couples should live when faced with setbacks and disillusionment. Whether it is a lack of money, conflict of some kind, or a job promotion, spouses are forced to make hard choices that could either result in them having a healthy marriage or becoming another divorce statistic. Unfortunately, people usually tend to believe that all problems immediately cease to exist at the altar.

They seem to think, as in fairy tales, that if they have vanquished the wicked witch or the evil stepmother—sorry, or mother-in-law—everything will be okay. However, anyone married for more than a few years can avow that this could not be further from the truth. Even the Scripture that says, "he who finds a wife finds a good thing" does not fail to remind us that "those who marry will face many troubles in this life" (Proverbs 18:22; 1 Corinthians 7:28). Regardless of one's ideology, marital life is challenging.

People need to learn how to handle both planned and unplanned challenges if their marriage is to work. This does not mean that desiring a "Happily Ever After" is wrong. However, marriage has much more to do with exhibiting attributes such as love, forgiveness, patience, understanding, compassion, and compromise than with fairytales. Issues and concerns, especially premarital ones, should be addressed outside of the legal bonds of marriage. Sadly, some couples make the mistake of discussing such matters after they have tied the knot, when delaying or calling off the wedding may have been a better solution.

According to 1 Peter 3:7, knowledge plays an enormous role in a couple's ability to build and sustain a loving relationship. Those relying on Rumpelstiltskin to spin straw into gold may be distressed to find out that there is no gold at the end of the day to pay the wedding bills, or for any of life's other necessities.

WEEK I: BEFORE MARRIAGE

UNDERSTANDING YOURSELF FIRST

> If you want to know someone better, asking them a question is still the best approach.

Nathaniel B. Carrington

Day 1: MY HUSBAND

Genesis 2:15 (NIV)

THE LORD GOD TOOK
THE MAN AND PUT HIM IN THE
GARDEN OF EDEN TO WORK IT
AND TAKE CARE OF IT.

Men: Are they really from Mars? Although the verdict is still out on this question, some have already concluded that they are. Unfortunately, characterizations conceived in the court of public opinion usually do not receive the scrutiny needed to validate their authenticity. Despite this fact, metaphors such as this are regularly used to describe the unexplainable behavior of some men towards their wives and families. As a result, "What does it mean to be a man?" is no longer garnering a straightforward answer from most quarters. Therefore, It's important that we do not allow ourselves to become complacent as the identity of our husbands, fathers, brothers, and sons is defamed. We can no longer allow ourselves to become overly susceptible to old wives' tales or new ideologies that depict men in an unfavorable light. As men, we must be willing to accept accountability for our own actions and proactively stand up for what the Bible refers to as true manliness. Such efforts can only prove beneficial to all, especially those ladies considering marriage and young men searching for mentors. Without such dialogue, we will continue to falter at attaining a real understanding of what it means to be a man.

So regardless of the chatter, if you want to know someone better, asking them a question is still the best approach. We can no longer cling to unfounded illusions or false standards set by people who think they know best. For the sake of our families and communities, we need to confront these untruths by participating in discussions built on reality instead of ambiguity. Cease the irresponsible and dishonest behavior that fuel misunderstanding. Stop avoiding the tough questions surrounding the subject, and provide clear and concise responses that create an honest dialogue about what it means to be manly. While this may seem like a tall order, being honest about our limitations and personal and professional inadequacies, and the willingness to change is all that is required.

Fortunately, the Scriptures have already answered some of the more pertinent questions relating to this subject. 1 Corinthians 13: 4-7 describes many of the characteristics of true love. Ephesians 5:25 compare the love between a man and woman to that of Christ and the church. Ephesians 6:4 describes the relationship between a father and his children. Ephesians 6:5-9 describes the appropriate work relationship between employees and employers. These verses all paint a reliable picture of how a man should function within his home, workplace, place of worship, and community as a servant-leader, provider, teacher, nurturer, and lover. Those needing practical examples should seek out the counsel of trustworthy men and women who has depicted such godly and illustrious virtues (Mathew 14:28-30).

Woman was made to be man's equal and not his subordinate, to rule with him and not be ruled by him.

Nathaniel B. Carrington

Day 2: MY WIFE

Genesis 2:18 (NIV)

THE LORD GOD SAID, "IT IS NOT GOOD FOR THE MAN TO BE ALONE. I WILL MAKE A HELPER SUITABLE FOR HIM.

Are women really from Venus? While some men hastily rush to answer this question, we should not be surprised if their answer is impeded by ladies saying, "We are not." From as far back as the First World War, women have always played a significant role in ensuring the success of their families. Unlike previous generations, today's modern women are attaining key positions in areas once solely dominated by men. The fact is, our culture is rapidly evolving, and women, as well as men, are changing with it. While there are situations that may place women in an unfavorable light, we should not allow these cases to cast a shadow on women's contributions throughout the years, especially those women who, regardless of their professional ambitions, remain loyal to their families and communities.

Instead of undermining these remarkable accomplishments, we should remember that there was a time in history when women were unable to vote, own land, or work outside the home. What they could or couldn't do was controlled by their husbands and in some cases the law of the land. Regrettably, women had no recourse to address the many injustices forced on them by others, including their husbands. Thus, many of them were treated as inferior, with little to offer the community outside of sex, child-bearing, and homemaking. What was first a practice soon became an expectation, and eventually, God's intended purpose for women was denied.

Scripture informs us that everything that God created was called good, except for man being alone (Genesis 2:28). As a result, God said, "I will make him a help meet for him" (Genesis 2:18). Unfortunately, this verse was taken out of context by many Christian and non-Christian individuals who thought it referred to women's servitude. A closer look at the same phase in Hebrew reveals that "help meet for him," *Ezer kenegdo*, means an equal but opposite helper to him. Viewing women in this light show that they were created to be much more than servants. God made man and women to function similarly to the two hands of the human body. Both were given the capacity to help each other fulfill each task assigned to them by God (Genesis 1:28).

The woman was made to be man's equal and not his subordinate, to rule with him and not be ruled by him. They were to function individually and collectively while fulfilling God's will on earth. Out of the Scriptures comes a picture of a woman who is noble, trustworthy, submissive, committed, industrious, godly, a homemaker, a mother, wise, fair, productive, blessed, praiseworthy, and honorable. The greatest of these merits is her love for her husband and her fear of the Lord (Proverbs 3:10-31). "It is not good that the man should be alone; I will make him a help meet fit for him" (Genesis 2:18).

> Having the support of a loving and healthy family environment is key to developing good relationship skills.
>
> Nathaniel B. Carrington

Day 3: MY IN-LAWS

Ruth 1:14 (NIV)

AT THIS, THEY WEPT ALOUD AGAIN. THEN ORPAH KISSED HER MOTHER-IN-LAW GOODBYE, BUT RUTH CLUNG TO HER.

While we could list some of the influences responsible for the traits we find so likable in our spouses, the contribution made by in-laws usually outweighs them. It is very likely that many of the qualities you fell in love with are similar to those of your in-laws—your spouse's relatives. Therefore, no matter how much we may deny it, no spouse has the sole claim to the word "self-made person." The fact is, history has proven that having the support of a loving and healthy family environment is key to developing good relationship skills. The same thing cannot be said for those raised in an unhealthy home. Spouses who actively cultivate a healthy relationship with their nuclear and extended family members usually benefit immensely from their advice and experience. The story of Naomi and her daughter-in-law Ruth is just one of the many examples of such a relationship. During their own personal loss in Moab, they were able to maintain their unique mother-daughter bond. The biblical writers were very transparent about the mutual respect that they had for each other (Ruth 3:1). Ruth's mother-in-law's affectionate influence was instrumental not only in helping her find a new home but also in helping her find a new husband.

When we review the impact of Ruth's choices on Judeo-Christianity, she is recorded as the great-grandmother of David (Matthew 1:5). As seen in the story of Ruth and Naomi, building a healthy relationship with one's in-laws can sometimes work out to everyone's advantage. And while this by no means guarantees that you will have the same outcome as Ruth and Naomi, you will never know if you don't try (Romans 12:18).

As mentioned before, in-laws who fail to develop healthy relationships usually find themselves walking on eggshells whenever they are in each other's company. One story that illustrates this is that of Jacob and his father-in-law, Laban. At the height of their contentious relationship, Jacob had to flee his home to secure his own life and his future. And while the story ends with both men signing a peace treaty, no mention is ever made of Laban having a change of heart about his feeling towards Jacob (Genesis 31:2). While some in-laws can be difficult to get along with, there is hope if both parties are willing to work through their differences (Proverbs 15:1). A word of wisdom to newlyweds: Not all problems experienced by couples are the result of their in-laws (Matthew 7:1-5).

Men Women Marriage
42 Days to Victorious Living

Love, and not money, should be the only reason why two people should walk down the aisle to spend the rest of their lives together.

Nathaniel B. Carrington

Day 4: MY RELIGION

Amos 3:3 (NIV)

DO TWO WALK TOGETHER UNLESS THEY HAVE AGREED TO DO SO?

2 Corinthians 6:14 (NIV)

DO NOT BE YOKED TOGETHER WITH UNBELIEVERS. FOR WHAT DO RIGHTEOUSNESS AND WICKEDNESS HAVE IN COMMON? OR WHAT FELLOWSHIP CAN LIGHT HAVE WITH DARKNESS?

What?! Are you still telling me that I shouldn't get married to my fiancé or my fiancée? We've already made the arrangements, rented the hall, fired a wedding planner and hired a new one, and contracted a French chef.

It's way too late to call things off—the contracts are already signed. We all know of that couple who considered calling it quits only weeks before the day of their wedding. However, they decided not to do so because of the amount of time and money already invested in the ceremony. Despite the differences in their beliefs, these individuals still succumbed to the pressure to say, "I do" when "I do not" may have been the more appropriate choice for them.

Love, and not money, should be the only reason why two people should walk down the aisle to spend the rest of their lives together. While money can be a great persuader, and according to the Bible "answereth all things," it usually does not work in such situations, at least not in the long term (Ecclesiastes 10:19). If two people are so evidently different that their communication is hampered, counseling, not marriage, should be the next step.

No matter how beautiful or elegant a wedding ceremony may be, having different religious views always leads to unexpected disagreements (1 Kings 11:4). This is not only true for couples but also for family members, relatives, and friends involved in the wedding. The challenges associated with being unequally yoked are intensified when marital conflict arises due to different lifestyles or religious beliefs. Spouses of differing religious persuasions sometimes even argue over which faith their child should be raised in, or school they should attend. The truth is, personal traits and choices that may be considered acceptable by some people may not sit well with your spouse, especially if these behaviors conflict with their convictions.

God never intended for marriage to be a place where spouses would be at war over doctrinal truths. It was His intention from the beginning that they would be united and governed by the same belief system (Mark 10:6-9). When a couple decides to submit to each other, as to God's word, the nature of the relationship begins to reflect the heart of God towards man (Jeremiah 29:11). On the other hand, if you are married to someone who does not share your religious views, there is still hope. 1 Peter 3 gives wives an approach that husbands in the same predicament would be wise to follow. "Wives, in the same way, submit yourselves to your own husbands so that, if any of them do not believe the word, they may be won over without words by the behavior of their wives, when they see the purity and reverence of your lives."

> We should never be duped into believing that the only way to true happiness is to "Keep up with Mr. and Ms. Jones
>
> **Nathaniel B. Carrington**

Day 5: MY OBLIGATIONS

Genesis 1:28 (NIV)

GOD BLESSED THEM AND SAID TO THEM, BE FRUITFUL AND INCREASE IN NUMBER; FILL THE EARTH AND SUBDUE IT. RULE OVER THE FISH IN THE SEA AND THE BIRDS IN THE SKY AND OVER EVERY LIVING CREATURE THAT MOVES ON THE GROUND."

In the Old Testament, a son, the firstborn, received the family inheritance in the advent of his father's absence, illness, or death. If there were only daughters and no males born to the family, the eldest daughter would become the successor (Joshua 17:3-6). Regardless of who was selected, male or female, the successor would be responsible for taking on the role of head of the family and fulfilling the obligations of the deceased father Genesis 24:36). While it was customary for the remaining family members to faithfully carry out their initial responsibilities, it was the heir's sole duty to ensure the family's survival. If he were successful, they would throw their full weight behind his leadership. If he were not, they would look elsewhere for a replacement. While such actions would be considered harsh by today's standards, it was not uncommon for a family to be sold into slavery if they were unable to fulfill their obligations.

While the role and the selection of the successor have evolved throughout the years, fulfilling specific innate family responsibilities continues to be a socioeconomic behavior that ensures the survival of the family unit. However, when these practices become nothing more than keeping up social appearances, then the original role of the successor is diminished. When this occurs, things usually become very unpleasant for the remaining family members who are forced to act like everything is all right even if it is not.

Therefore, careful examination of one's family structure should be done before deciding on which obligations should be fulfilled. It reminds me of the old idiom "Keeping up with the Joneses." My late mother would always explain it this way to me. "What may bring your neighbor happiness, may bring you tears." Following in her footsteps, what may work for one family, may not work for yours. If you can "keep up with the Joneses," and still have a healthy marriage, maybe you should continue. However, if doing so begin to erode the very foundation of your relationships, then it would be wise to cease such endeavors. We should never be duped into believing that the only way to true happiness is to "Keep up with Mr. and Mrs. Jones." In fact, most people who have gotten to know them quite well would attest that pursuing such a quest could lead to misery instead of happiness. While there are enormous material benefits to be had, the stress and anxiety seen on the faces of friends and loved ones sometimes tell a different story (2 Timothy 2:4). If your mate or children are suffering unnecessarily because of your many obligations, it may be wise to reevaluate their importance to you and your family. Those on the other hand that lead to the health and posterity of your family should be kept (Genesis 2:15-18).

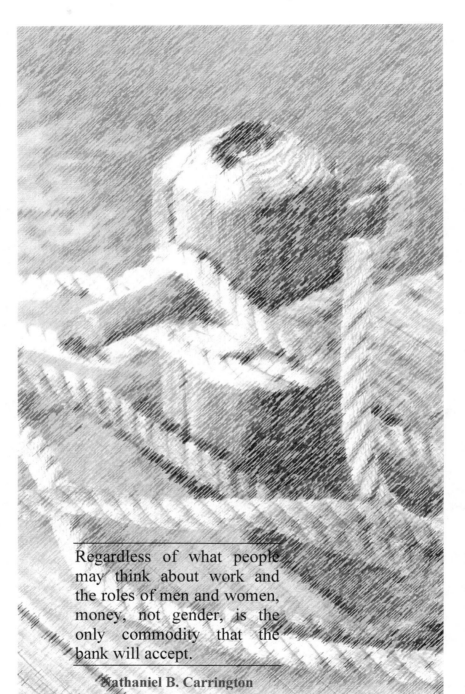

> Regardless of what people may think about work and the roles of men and women, money, not gender, is the only commodity that the bank will accept.
>
> Nathaniel B. Carrington

Day 6: MY WORK

1 Timothy 5:8 (NIV)

ANYONE WHO DOES NOT PROVIDE FOR THEIR RELATIVES, AND ESPECIALLY FOR THEIR OWN HOUSEHOLD, HAS DENIED THE FAITH AND IS WORSE THAN AN UNBELIEVER.

Who is wearing the pants in the family? Whenever people ask this question, they are usually referring to the person making most of the decisions in the relationship. However, if the individual exercising controlling authority in a household is a woman, the man is viewed as less manly. While men have always taken on this role, the contribution of women throughout the years in securing the wellbeing of their families cannot be denied.

This was a lesson that couples learned only too well during the global economic crisis of 2008. The possible loss of income due to growing job insecurity became a reality equally shared by both men and women. The job conditions at that time offered little to no assurance of regular employment. As a result, people who lost their jobs or couldn't find work had to learn to juggle familiar and unfamiliar tasks to meet their family responsibilities. For some this meant going back to school to get a degree, working two jobs to offset financial shortfalls, starting one or two small businesses, or volunteering their skills to an organization as a means of gaining needed job experience or exposure.

Unfortunately, while most of these measures were successful at addressing the income issues, they did little to help the social ones. Nevertheless, working men and women with their backs against the wall were forced to rethink and take on gender-specific roles that weren't traditional for their gender. The instability created conditions that reinforced what many mature couples had already known all along. And that is, it doesn't matter who is working if the family income is enough to meet its current needs. For many people during the crisis, if that meant that the lady would be wearing the pants, the only concerns were the size, fit, and color. Unlike previous generations, regardless of what people may think about work and the roles of men and women, money, not gender, is the only commodity that the bank will accept. Our parents' famous words "unless that man has a job or is in the process of getting one, do not get married to him" is still good advice. However, the number of women breaking the glass ceiling within the workplace undermines this argument a bit. The fact is, today's women are involved in almost every aspect of the home, including being the breadwinner. Because of this, both men and women have a realistic opportunity to learn how to share this godly responsibility equally (Proverbs 31:10-31).

So, whatever the causes may be in today's culture, both men and women are now responsible for the success of their household. While these changes can lead to some confusion as to who is responsible for making the financial decisions in the relationship, it does not lessen the role of the man as the provider and head. "But I would have you know, that the head of every man is Christ; and the head of the woman [is] the man; and the head of Christ is God" (1 Corinthians 11:3).

> Retrospection is usually best for separating infatuation from facts when making life-changing decisions.
>
> **Nathaniel B. Carrington**

Day 7: MY MATURITY

Proverbs 1:4-5 (NIV)

TO GIVE PRUDENCE TO THE NAIVE,
TO THE YOUTH KNOWLEDGE AND DISCRETION,
A WISE MAN WILL HEAR AND INCREASE IN
LEARNING, AND A MAN OF UNDERSTANDING
WILL ACQUIRE WISE COUNSEL,

I think by now we all know that maturity is much more than just driving a new car, wearing a new suit, staying out past midnight, or even giving or receiving your first kiss. Contrary to what many believe, maturity is the ability to respond to life's challenges with a learned behavior instead of an impulsive or emotional one. This brings to mind a conversation that I had with a group of parents about the lack of maturity being exhibited by our teenagers and young adults. As we realized what that would mean for future generations of young couples, we knew that we had to step up and do something about it. The problem was that no one knew what to do or where to start.

Our thoughts were soon brought to a standstill when one parent mentioned that the Merriam-Webster Dictionary stated that "people are legally considered to have reached maturity at the age of 18 in the United States." I remembered thinking to myself, and saying out loud at the same time, "there is a difference between being old enough to write a check legally, and writing or using one correctly." While this may come as a surprise to most children, parents, based on their own experience, know only too well the problems that a lack of maturity can create. Retrospection is usually best for separating infatuation from facts when making life-changing decisions. Unfortunately, each generation of young people that comes along usually pays little attention to the advice given to them by their elders.

We have all made the mistake of believing that age and maturity unequivocally go together (1 Corinthians 6:12). Regrettably, we still do the same thing when selecting a mate. Instead of relying on time-tested qualities such as trust, commitment, and love, we allow questionable ideologies to guide our choice. Acting maturely in a marriage can enable a couple to manage life's challenges in a manner that maintains a stable and healthy household. While some couples choose at their own peril to overlook this truth, others only know too well the hurt and pain that can be experienced by doing so. This philosophy is deeply embedded in the Christian belief that loving ones spouse to the point of laying down your life is maturity demonstrated at its best (John 15:13).

Men Women Marriage
42 Days to Victorious Living

WEEK II: AFTER MARRIAGE

LIVING OUT THE ESSENTIALS

Day 8: TWO BECOME ONE

Mark 10:6-8 (NIV)

BUT AT THE BEGINNING OF CREATION GOD 'MADE THEM MALE AND FEMALE. FOR THIS REASON, A MAN WILL LEAVE HIS FATHER AND MOTHER AND BE UNITED TO HIS WIFE, AND THE TWO WILL BECOME ONE FLESH.' SO THEY ARE NO LONGER TWO, BUT ONE FLESH.

The phrase never the twain shall meet suggest "two things are too different to exist alongside each other." Imagine telling your future wife or husband something similar about the two of you, while at the same time conveying your undying love for them. Some relationship specialists might see such a statement as contradictory, not the words of a person enjoying a healthy and vibrant relationship. However, before we are too quick to judge this situation, do you recall the first time your wife came to you with the idea of dressing in matching outfits? What may have seemed to be an over-the-top idea was in her eyes an expression of how she felt about her marriage. Despite many chuckles, I can remember my wife glowing with a sense of pride as we both strolled together down the street in the same outfit.

To my astonishment, what was a one-time request soon became a public declaration symbolizing our unity. While an outward expression of love cannot make a couple one, it is common to see persons using such symbols to show belonging or togetherness. Therefore, regardless of the differences in a person's traits or ethnicity, dressing in similar apparel can gives the impression of uniformity. Scripture would seem to suggest that God's method of making us one flesh shares a similar approach.

The only difference is that it encourages us to add to our earthy garments spiritual ones. As 1 Peter 3:3-4 says, "Your beauty should not come from outward adornments such as elaborate hairstyles and the wearing of gold jewelry or fine clothes. Rather, it should be that of your inner self, the unfading beauty of a gentle and quiet spirit, which is of great worth in God's sight." God's holy garments unite couples in the same manner as a husband and wife's matching outfits. His word provides both spouses with guidelines on how to fulfill this marital command. It tells us that Christ is the matching outfits for the husband and wife (Romans 13:14). The fabrics are made of the word of God (John 1:1). And we dress in these garments when we obey Jesus' command to "love one another, even as I have loved you" (John 13:35). Next time you step out in matching apparels, pay no attention to the chuckles of those standing in the shadows. Smile, it is not your similarities or matching garments that matters. It is your willingness to submit to God's word as one (John 17:22).

Men Women Marriage

42 Days to Victorious Living

Inconsiderate behavior in any form can lead to uneasy feelings in any marriage

Nathaniel B. Carrington

Day 9: RESPECT

Ephesians 5:33 (NIV)

HOWEVER, EACH ONE OF YOU ALSO MUST LOVE HIS WIFE AS HE LOVES HIMSELF, AND THE WIFE MUST RESPECT HER HUSBAND.

How can I respect a man or a woman who has no respect for themselves? This is a question that is often asked by persons who face similar issues. While there are many destructive marital behaviors, this one seems to top the list of offenders. An inconsiderate word, an offensive look, and the dissemination of private matters are all examples of disrespectful behavior. For troubled relationships, such actions can be "the straw that breaks the camel's back." Newlyweds, on the other hand, may see them as regular communication challenges. Regardless of the number of years in their marriage, if you ask a couple a question about such an issue, you will most likely hear "we never saw it coming," or "we did not know that it existed in our relationship." Today's couples are so busy trying to cope with the stresses of life that they fail to recognize the impolite attitudes seeping into their communication. I once heard a spouse say, "my husband doesn't care about my feelings."

Further introspection revealed that it was the rude way that he responded that made her feel that way. It wasn't too long before the husband confessed that his actions stemmed from his wife's refusal to dance with him at an alumni event. His emotional description of the incident was so vivid that it felt like it occurred only a few days before we had the discussion. A second introspection revealed that instead of listening to each other, they were misled into believing that airing their dirty laundry in public would somehow settle the matter.

The fact is, inconsiderate behavior in any form can lead to uneasy feelings in any marriage. When asked about the way they were acting towards each other, they responded by saying, "I was only trying to get my spouse to understand how I felt." They each believed that they might somehow be swayed if they saw how many persons disagreed with their position. I remember saying to them that communicating loaded messages, unintentionally or intentionally, can come across as a personal attack. While help from close friends and family can bring a sense of sanity, it does not make the marriage impermeable to criticism. In such an environment, even trivial issues can be blown out of proportion. If you are faced with similar problems in your marriage, seeking godly professional help, especially if you are unable to resolve it on your own, might be the right thing to do (Ephesians 5:21)

Men Women Marriage
42 Days to Victorious Living

> Ultimately, the Scriptures never intended for submission to be used as a means of controlling others, especially our spouses.
>
> **Nathaniel B. Carrington**

Day 10: SUBMISSION

Ephesians 5:21-24 (NIV)

SUBMIT TO ONE ANOTHER OUT OF REVERENCE FOR CHRIST. WIVES, SUBMIT YOURSELVES TO YOUR OWN HUSBANDS AS YOU DO TO THE LORD. FOR THE HUSBAND IS THE HEAD OF THE WIFE AS CHRIST IS THE HEAD OF THE CHURCH, HIS BODY, OF WHICH HE IS THE SAVIOR. NOW AS THE CHURCH SUBMITS TO CHRIST, SO ALSO WIVES SHOULD SUBMIT TO THEIR HUSBANDS IN EVERYTHING.

Submission: the word alone causes me to wonder what the Apostle Paul was thinking about when he wrote this. There has never been a more misunderstood passage of

Scripture by men and women of every race and culture. However, we should not forget that scriptures must be spiritually discerned (1 Corinthians 2:14). I remember when my wife and I were having our first Bible study together. Her first response after I introduced her to Ephesians 5:21-33 was to just stare at me. In my excitement as a young husband, I forgot that most people pay more attention to your motives, not your words. So, on our second Bible study, I committed myself to explaining what "all things" meant to me, and listening to what it meant to her. Some of the words coming out of our conversation were obedience, compliance, surrender, and giving in.

Considering these words, it is not surprising how many spouses respond when asked to submit: Who do you think you are? You are not my boss, father, or mother. You cannot tell me what to do. I am my own man or woman. If we are to be honest, many of us have heard these same words from our wife, husband, children, or even office subordinates. Why is submission such a struggle, for men and women? If we look back at our childhood, many of us would agree that submitting to our parents was not easy. While we were given more leverage as we got older, being told to be home before midnight still ruffled our feathers.

So, we can all agree that being asked to submit is challenging (1 John 3:16).

Ultimately, the Scriptures never intended for submission to be used as a means of controlling others, especially our spouses. Instead, it aimed to act as a loving deterrent for couples, families, and organizations to make wise decisions. Healthy submission has always produced a healthy socioeconomic environment for both secular and spiritual entities (Ephesians 5:22). Unfortunately, because of our inability to grasp this truth, rebellion and disobedience become the only alternatives. Jesus exemplified the correct behavior towards his heavenly Father (John 6:38). However, because of the many evils that are done in the name of submission, we should not forget the biblical clause "as you do to the Lord" (Ephesians 5:22). Therefore, the author believes that any decision to submit should be first evaluated by the Scriptures. When this is done correctly, understanding the enormous benefits of submission to a husband and wife is invaluable (Ephesians 5:21).

> We should never assume that we know what service means to our spouse. Instead, we should ask them, and maybe, if we are lucky enough, they might just tell us
>
> **Nathaniel B. Carrington**

Day 11: SERVICE

John 13:5 (NIV)

AFTER THAT, HE POURED WATER INTO A BASIN AND BEGAN TO WASH HIS DISCIPLES' FEET, DRYING THEM WITH THE TOWEL THAT WAS WRAPPED AROUND HIM.

No matter what a person's status in life may be, they can sometimes find themselves in a position where they need assistance. While this can be an uncomfortable feeling, it often provides well-intentioned persons with the opportunity to be of service to someone in need. The Bible shares this same sentiment by pointing out that helping others is the purest reflection of God's love for mankind

(Mark 10:44-45 and John 3:16). Imagine what would happen if more couples began to treat each other in this same manner, choosing not to look at their weaknesses as an impediment, but seeing them instead as opportunities for serving each other within their relationship. This supports what the Apostle Paul had to say about the way a husband should treat his wife (1 Peter 3:7).

According to these teachings, the husband has the unique opportunity and spiritual mandate to create an environment that serves the needs of the relationship. And while this can prove at times to be an uphill battle, he is responsible for helping his wife in a manner that reflects the Scriptures (Ephesians 5:28-29). Regardless of the inclination to follow the self-centered practices of our culture, serving each other should be held in high esteem by couples.

Unfortunately, fewer individuals are accepting this truth, and many are instead turning their sights solely towards material assets to meet the needs of their spouses (Ephesians 5:21-33). Many diligently work three to four jobs to acquire the prestigious house on the hill and two cars parked in the driveway. Imagine the astonishment on the face of a husband who has been told that if he provides everything for his wife, she will automatically be happy. Yet when all is said and done, he is still told, "you don't spend enough time with me."

What did we miss? Didn't we do the right thing? Why are we still being told we don't care? Maybe if we stop listening to everyone for just one second and actually listen to our spouse, we would hear what service really means to them. "You don't spend enough time with me, you no longer bring me flowers, cook me a special dinner, or go for those special walks." We somehow seem to forget that we were the one that our spouse fell in love with, not the houses or the cars. While some of these things are important, they pale in comparison to spending time with the one that you love. We should never assume that we know what service means to our spouse. Instead, we should ask them, and maybe, if we are lucky enough, they might just tell us (1 Peter 3:7).

Men Women Marriage
42 Days to Victorious Living

> Outside of the challenges associated with marital failures, such as infidelity, addictions, and other dubious behaviors, sex should be satisfying.
>
> **Nathaniel B. Carrington**

Day 12: SEX

Hebrews 13:4 (NIV)

MARRIAGE SHOULD BE HONORED BY ALL, AND THE MARRIAGE BED KEPT PURE, FOR GOD WILL JUDGE THE ADULTERER AND ALL THE SEXUALLY IMMORAL.

Sex: Could this be one of the reasons why we are experiencing problems in our relationship? I mean, how complicated can it get? This issue is discussed on television and in blogs, schools, churches, cafeterias—you name it, sex is everywhere. There was even a TV sitcom called "Sex and the City." This TV show gave viewers, especially women, personal insight into what their contemporaries were thinking and saying about this subject.

All this information, and still, many couples are experiencing significant challenges enjoying a healthy sex life. I personally believe that there is no easy answer to why this is happening. Some professionals have tried to address these issues by educating couples on various aspects of the subject, such as sexual, emotional, intellectual, and spiritual intimacy.

While this information has proven quite helpful for some, others have been unable to apply it to their everyday lives. So, to simplify this issue, let us reset the clock on the conversation. Outside of the challenges associated with marital failures, such as infidelity, addictions, and other dubious behaviors, sex should be satisfying. In other words, a healthy relationship equals a healthy sex life.

So, what should you do when you are having sexual problems in your relationship? While the Bible is not as vivid as secular sources, it does provide the reader with a few pertinent pointers that can help them navigate these sensitive issues. The Song of Solomon, one of the major books in the Bible, outlines several healthy stimulating behaviors and communications that could help add spice to any couple's relationship (Song of Solomon 4). While some of the language used may seem a bit over-expressive in some religious circles, the exchange of such words between two married persons can still be considered appropriate. While the gaps between spiritual and sexual intimacy may be a stretch for some Christians, marriage involves sexual activity between a man and a woman. In fact, the Bible states that "the husband should fulfill his marital duty to his wife, and likewise the wife to her husband. The wife does not have authority over her own body but yields it to her husband. In the same way, the husband does not have authority over his own body but yields it to his wife" (1 Corinthians 7:3-5). The fact is, despite the many worldly influences, "marriage is honorable in all, and the bed undefiled" (Hebrews 13:4).

Men Women Marriage

42 Days to Victorious Living

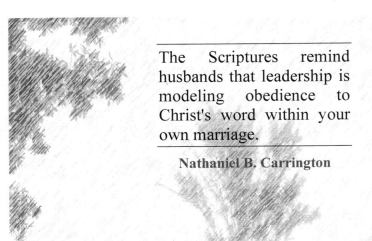

The Scriptures remind husbands that leadership is modeling obedience to Christ's word within your own marriage.

Nathaniel B. Carrington

Day 13: LEADERSHIP

Ephesians 5:25 (NIV)

HUSBANDS, LOVE YOUR WIVES, JUST AS CHRIST LOVED THE CHURCH AND GAVE HIMSELF UP FOR HER.

During the early part of our marriage, my wife and I found ourselves, like so many other anxious young couples, conversing about the importance of leadership. Without any hesitation, I automatically conveyed to my wife that as the man in the family, I would be the one who would be ultimately responsible for performing this duty. Regardless of my strong convictions, we knew that as a Christian couple, it was not prudent to follow any ideology that the Scriptures did not support. While our study of the Word confirmed that the husband was God's choice to be the head of the family, how he would perform that role was still not evident to us. One Scripture that guided us in the right direction was 1 Corinthians 11:23. This Scripture stated: "The head of every man is Christ, and the head of the woman is man, and the head of Christ is God." Seeing the institution of marriage from this perspective allowed us to view it as part of a larger hierarchical structure, God is the head. Christ's relationship with his Father was one of total surrender. Scripture recorded him saying, "By myself, I can do nothing" (John 5:30). In fact, before he was crucified, he said, "yet not my will, but yours be done" (Luke 22:42).

To Christ, being a good leader to his disciples meant obeying his Father's every word. By exhibiting this behavior, Christ affirmed that "the head of Christ is God." How, then, should the husband adjust his leadership style to affirm that "the head of every man is Christ"? Similar to Christ's relationship with his Father, we as Christians are reminded by the Scriptures that we cannot do anything without Jesus (John 15:5). Unlike the Merriam-Webster Dictionary, which describes leadership as "the power or ability to lead other people," the Scriptures remind husbands that leadership is modeling obedience to Christ's word within your own marriage. This lines up with the Scripture that commands, "Wives, submit yourselves to your own husbands as you do to the Lord" (Ephesians 5:22).

A wife's submission to her husband, therefore, requires that the husband first submits to Christ, as mentioned above, in the hierarchical structure. When my wife and I first had the conversation about leadership, my first response was based on what I had heard from both Christian and secular culture. However, now that I have acquired a better idea of what the Scriptures expect before I ask her to follow me, I will ensure that I am doing my utmost to follow Christ's words. The Apostle Paul said, "Follow my example, as I follow the example of Christ" (1 Corinthians 11:1).

Men Women Marriage
42 Days to Victorious Living

> Decisions, no matter the intentions, have consequences.
> Assessing the pros and cons before making them is always the wisest thing to do.
>
> **Nathaniel B. Carrington**

Nathaniel B. Carrington

Day 14: DECISIONS

1 Corinthians 1:10 (NIV)

I APPEAL TO YOU, BROTHERS AND SISTERS, IN THE NAME OF OUR LORD JESUS CHRIST, THAT ALL OF YOU AGREE WITH ONE ANOTHER IN WHAT YOU SAY AND THAT THERE BE NO DIVISIONS AMONG YOU, BUT THAT YOU BE PERFECTLY UNITED IN MIND AND THOUGHT.

Just recently my wife and I had a conversation with our children about attending college. While our youngest son was intrigued by the idea, the older ones seemed to be more excited about living on campus instead of off. As for us, all we could think about was whether they were ready to leave home. More important, because college is a life-changing event, we felt that it was necessary to discuss the possible challenges involved in making such a serious decision. While we were confident about their ability to get into college, because of the growing cost of college, avoiding debt would be difficult and in some cases impossible. Our children, with our help, would have to manage unplanned expenses, student materials, and other miscellaneous costs acquired while living on or off campus. What disquieted us was that our children didn't seem to be concerned about these challenges.

Moreover, they indicated that this exercise might be just jumping the gun, and unprofitable at the moment. In their own minds, they had more than enough time to prepare for college. Nevertheless, we informed them that decisions, no matter the intentions, have consequences and assessing the cost before making them is always the wisest thing to do. Their ability to meet the social, safety, academic, and transportation needs of college would ultimately determine how ready they were to attend, regardless of whether they were living at home or on campus (Matthew 19:26).

Marriage is no different from college, and therefore, overlooking its challenges is not wise, either (1 Peter 3:7). No matter how well thought through a plan may be, good situations can still go south. That unexpected job loss, sudden death, or inability to pay the rent or mortgage doesn't mean that you made the wrong decision. As most mature persons would put it, "life happens." How you respond when you can't make ends meet is what matters. So, regardless of how confident you may be, strive to make the most well-informed decision, and trust God to bring you through any unforeseen circumstances that may arise (Psalm 55:22).

Men Women Marriage
42 Days to Victorious Living

WEEK III: RESPONSIBILITIES

DISCOVERING YOUR ROLE

Marriage is much more than just meeting expectations.

Nathaniel B. Carrington

Day 15: EXPECTATIONS

Jeremiah 29:11 (NIV)

FOR I KNOW THE PLANS
I HAVE FOR YOU, DECLARES THE LORD, PLANS
TO PROSPER YOU AND NOT TO HARM YOU, PLANS
TO GIVE YOU HOPE AND A FUTURE.

The Merriam-Webster Dictionary defines "expectation" as "a feeling or belief about how successful, good, etc. someone or something will be." While many of us, including yours truly, have subscribed on numerous occasions to this belief, life has taught me that achieving one's expectations does not always chalk up to what people said it would be. Unfortunately, some couples are terrified by the knowledge that they will not be able to meet certain expectations within their marriage. I remember as a child idolizing the character of Mr. Ingalls, played by Michael Landon, on the TV show "Little House on the Prairie." Even then, I envied the loving relationship that Mr. Ingalls shared with his TV wife and children, especially Laura, the bright-eyed, freckle-faced girl who captured the hearts of all avid lovers of the show. His continuous efforts to better himself and his family embodied all the godly characteristics that I believe a father should have.

This also held true for his wife, Caroline, played by Karen Grassle. Her calm and soothing persona usually brought out the best in Mr. Ingalls. While the two characters portrayed a beautiful example of a harmonious relationship, too little of the show focused on some of the more challenging aspects of marriage. Whether it was the producer's fault or my own, I seem only to recall those moments of the TV show that placed each spouse in their best light. Imagine how astonished I was when I realized that real-life relationships are much more challenging than fictional TV ones.

Marriage is much more than just meeting expectations. While the feelings that arise from a couple accomplishing their goals can be quite satisfying, the opposite can be just as devastating. The Bible encourages us to trust God in every situation, including marriage (Philippians 4:12). Any mature couple will testify that the secret to their happiness and longevity is learning to be faithful to each other, even when expectations are not met.

Like Mr. Ingalls, we all have a mental list of hopes and dreams that we believe would be inevitable if we could just attain true happiness. Marriage is a real-life institution consisting of a man and woman's relationship. It is highly unlikely that either one will get everything that they desire. It starts with a promise and is sealed with the words "to have and to hold, from this day forward, for better, for worse, for richer, for poorer, in sickness or in health, to love and to cherish 'till death do us part, I do.

Men Women Marriage
42 Days to Victorious Living

Doing nothing while crying over one's predicament does little to help anyone

Nathaniel B. Carrington

Day 16: FINANCES

Matthew 6:33 (NIV)

BUT SEEK FIRST HIS KINGDOM AND HIS RIGHTEOUSNESS, AND ALL THESE THINGS WILL BE GIVEN TO YOU AS WELL.

While many Christian couples are still struggling with their consciences as they relate to the love of money, Ecclesiastes 10:19 reminds us that "money answereth all things." No matter how much we may try to avoid this subject, it is evident that there is a strong correlation between a family's standard of living and the financial health of the economy. As mentioned previously, this reality was made only too clear when several persons were forced to deal with the uncomfortable feeling of losing their livelihoods and homes because of the volatility in the market. What do you do when your finances are in chaos, and your boss tells you, " last in, first out"? The outcome of such news can prove quite devastating for a newlywed with a growing family, especially when you start to realize that some people judged you more on what you possess than what you confess. Regardless, getting by on one income while going without your basic needs being met can be challenging.

Fortunately, the Bible gives those who find themselves in such a situation hope when it says, "life does not consist in an abundance of possessions" (Luke 12:15). So, downsizing to one car, learning to live on a limited budget, and cutting back on eating out are some of the many practices that can help a family adjust to their new norm. In addition to these changes, deciding to resist some of the things that this culture deems necessary is also very helpful when implementing good budgeting practices. When individuals understand that you do not have to "keep up with the Joneses" to have a happy home, adjusting to such changes is less stressful.

As couples, we should try our best not to allow our financial struggles to overwhelm us as we manage our daily affairs. Instead, we should focus on our immediate needs and not blindly run after unnecessary material possessions. We should never forget what our priestly heritage teaches us about giving (Matthew 6:25-34). Making the hard decision to be a blessing to someone else while trusting God to meet our daily needs is a part of the Christian belief (2 Kings 4). However, doing nothing while crying over one's predicament does little to help anyone.

Realistically, some of us, if not all, will suffer from financial difficulties at some time in our life (Genesis 12:10). Therefore, we should make every effort to put our trust in God's word and sovereign will, and not our own strength. As the saying goes, "little with contentment is great gain."

Men Women Marriage
42 Days to Victorious Living

Children are usually not emotionally ready to understand or cope with adult problems

Nathaniel B. Carrington

Day 17: CHILDREN

Ephesians 6:1-4 (NIV)

CHILDREN, OBEY YOUR PARENTS IN THE LORD, FOR THIS IS RIGHT. "HONOR YOUR FATHER AND MOTHER" WHICH IS THE FIRST COMMANDMENT WITH A PROMISE "SO THAT IT MAY GO WELL WITH YOU AND THAT YOU MAY ENJOY LONG LIFE ON THE EARTH." FATHERS, DO NOT EXASPERATE YOUR CHILDREN; INSTEAD, BRING THEM UP IN THE TRAINING AND INSTRUCTION OF THE LORD.

Some psychologists say that the needs of a child outweigh those of a parent. While I somewhat agree, having children of my own, I don't believe that they should always be the primary focus. This is especially true when parents are experiencing various challenges in their marriage. Those who have traveled on a plane know that before leaving the ground, parents are instructed in the event of turbulence to put on their oxygen mask before attending to their children.

As a parent myself, I can understand why we, and not the child, are given this grave responsibility. The child's level of maturity and capacity to follow instructions are just a few things that come to mind. On the other hand, while some children are good at carrying out their duties, parents should not rely too heavily on them to do so, especially in times of crisis (1 Corinthians 13:11). I believe this same principle applies to couples experiencing turbulence in their marriage.

Young children and even older ones are usually not emotionally ready to understand or cope with adult problems. Therefore, couples should proceed with caution whenever talking to their children about the challenges in their marriage. Failure to do this can make matters worse, not only for the parent but also for the siblings, who may already be struggling with their own rivalry. One couple from the Bible who were prime examples of this dysfunction was Isaac and Rebecca. Their indecisiveness over which sons should lead the family resulted in a lifelong family conflict. The first incident led to the younger brother Jacob deceiving his older brother out of his birthright and then the family blessings. His self-seeking actions caused him to flee his parents' home to avoid his brother Esau's anger (Genesis 27:41). It should be no surprise to anyone where Jacob got his talent for deception from (Genesis 25:13).

Today's child psychologists seem to agree that "children learn mostly by what they see, and not by what they hear." The dysfunctional behaviors modeled by parents can sometimes be interpreted as normal by their children. No wonder the Bible says, "Train up your children in the love and in the fear of the Lord." If we as parents do that, they will have had an example to follow in times of crisis (Proverbs 22:6).

Men Women Marriage

42 Days to Victorious Living

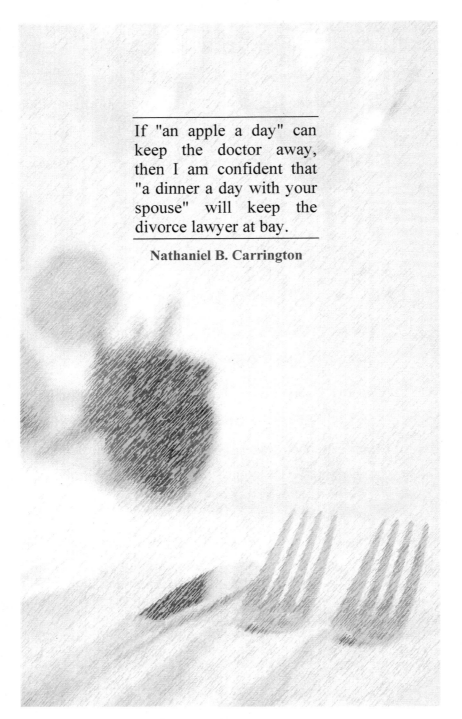

If "an apple a day" can keep the doctor away, then I am confident that "a dinner a day with your spouse" will keep the divorce lawyer at bay.

Nathaniel B. Carrington

Nathaniel B. Carrington

Day 18: FOOD

1 Corinthians 10:31 (NIV)

SO WHETHER YOU EAT OR
DRINK OR WHATEVER YOU DO,
DO IT ALL FOR THE GLORY OF GOD.

I never understood the close-knit relationship that existed between food and love until I went on my first romantic dinner-date. It was not the dinner that left me feeling on top of the world, but the fact that it gave me the opportunity to spend some quality time with a person that I cared for. While it took me one month to save enough money to pay for the dinner, I can still remember hearing myself saying, "it was worth every penny." Asking a person, "Would you mind going out to dinner with me?" seems to be the most natural thing to do when you find yourself attracted to someone. Many of us can still remember how nervous we were while going on our first date with our now husband or wife. I am sure that it didn't come as a surprise to anyone when we told them that most of the time was spent staring at each other, instead of eating the food that gradually went cold on the table.

The fact that we were still smiling as the waiter anxiously gave us the pricey check only reaffirms how special these moments were. Even couples who reserve a moment at home for a romantic dinner together experience the same ecstatic feeling as those at a prestigious restaurant. Sadly, many couples, because of their tight schedule, no longer put aside time to enjoy each other while digesting a lovely meal. While both my wife and I are guilty of such behavior, we still found time to plan many home-cooked dinners while the kids were asleep. Dinners that we both found quite delicious, and I am not just talking about food. If "an apple a day" can keep the doctor away, then I am confident that "a dinner a day" with your spouse will keep the divorce lawyer at bay.

Taking time out to show your spouse how much you appreciate the effort they put into preparing a romantic meal is always a welcome gesture. Criticizing their cooking, on the other hand, will only send them the wrong message, and that is that you neither enjoyed their presence or the dinner. Such harsh words can only change the mood at any dinner table from one of optimism to one of pessimism. If you had to ask any couple what made their dinner so special, they would most likely tell you that it was not the food or location, but the time spent together.

Romantic dinner dates provide individuals with an opportunity to communicate how serious they are about getting to know each other. It can also be used to inform them of your hopes and dreams for the relationship. If you are still having a difficult time understanding the impact that food can have on a relationship, consider the profits being made by most fast-food restaurants in America. It is not only the kids doing the ordering, but also dozens of husbands or wives standing alone doing the same thing (Proverbs 11:25).

Men Women Marriage

42 Days to Victorious Living

Godly dressing starts with the word modesty.

Nathaniel B. Carrington

Day 19: APPAREL

Romans 12 (NIV)

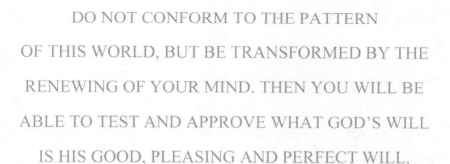

DO NOT CONFORM TO THE PATTERN OF THIS WORLD, BUT BE TRANSFORMED BY THE RENEWING OF YOUR MIND. THEN YOU WILL BE ABLE TO TEST AND APPROVE WHAT GOD'S WILL IS HIS GOOD, PLEASING AND PERFECT WILL.

Do you have a problem with my dress? Is it too long, or is it too short? Does my dress fit my gender? These are some of the many questions that most men and women ask themselves when something is said about the outfit they are wearing. As a young teenager, I found myself caught between two generations. Those my parents' age paid closer attention to what they wore as Christians. They believed that their dress reflected their faith, and therefore, it was consequential that what they said and wore affirmed their convictions. We, the younger generation at that time, were beginning to entertain the idea of wearing outfits that reflected more of our personality and culture, and less of our faith. And while the older generation felt somewhat uncomfortable with the way we were dressing; the margin of difference was relatively minor. Unlike today's younger generation, the primary concern of that day was centered around not wearing garments worn by the opposite gender.

As years passed, these standards became more and more relaxed, especially as persons began experiencing different cultures and climates. I remember one incident that occurred in the church I attended when I was just a kid. One of the holy ladies mentioned that while traveling abroad and experiencing zero-degree temperature, she had no choice but to dress in men's slacks. We, the church, never stopped to sympathize with her predicament, but immediately scolded her for wearing men's garments. We never considered the fact that it was "zero" degrees. In other words, it was unbearably cold for someone coming from a warm climate. Today, I can honestly say that I finally understand what godly dress means and that It starts with the word modesty.

The Merriam-Webster defines modesty as the quality of behaving, and especially dressing, in ways that do not attract sexual attention. While this may have little to do with wearing your dress length down to your ankles or up to your neck, if anyone is overemphasizing the sexual parts of their anatomy, then they are not dressing modestly (1 Timothy 2:9).

Men Women Marriage
42 Days to Victorious Living

The malicious use of words can have devastating effects, not only on the originator but also on the listener and the person being slandered

Nathaniel B. Carrington

Day 20: PRIVACY

Psalm 55:12-13 (NIV)

IF AN ENEMY WERE INSULTING ME, I COULD ENDURE IT; IF A FOE WERE RISING AGAINST ME, I COULD HIDE. BUT IT IS YOU, A MAN LIKE MYSELF, MY COMPANION, MY CLOSE FRIEND,

How much of your personal or professional life should you share with others? Is the information too sensitive for the listener? Should you even be sharing any of your friends' or family's personal issues at all? I have often found myself sitting alone at my desk asking these questions while preparing for a Sunday sermon or a counseling session. While I am cautious with the content of my own communication, at times, I find a need to intentionally draw comparisons from my own life circumstances, to better relate to those of others. Unfortunately, there is a downside to any individual becoming so transparent. As speakers, we should be careful not to forget that information shared in a public arena is no longer private. In other words, it no longer belongs to you and thus can be dispersed in any manner that the listener deems appropriate.

While the thought of this happening may seem irrelevant to many in this new digital world of social networking, the statement that "sticks and stones may break my bones, but words will never hurt me" is still false. If there is one thing that history has taught us, is that the malicious use of words can have devastating effects, not only on the originator but also on the listener and the person being slandered (James 3:4-6).

Thus, it is necessary that we limit what we share not only about ourselves but also about others. This principle holds true for marriage as well. While couples often need help in working through their challenges, deciding whom you can trust to share your marital issues with can be a challenge (James 5:16). One practice that my wife and I found quite helpful in achieving this early in our marriage was when we realized that there is a difference between acquaintances and confidants.

People in your life whom you know but who are not your close friends are your acquaintances. You should be very careful what you share with them. On the other hand, people that you know personally, and trust are your confidants. You may be able to share more in-depth detail about your marriage with them. Unfortunately, because people's motives and intentions are not always clear, we should continually seek God to lead us to those individuals who are mature enough to help us resolve our issues privately (Proverbs 12:26).

Men Women Marriage

42 Days to Victorious Living

When a person is no longer able to manage their challenges, it is time to seek godly counsel.

Nathaniel B. Carrington

Day 21: COUNSELING

Isaiah 1:18 (NIV)

"COME NOW, LET US SETTLE THE MATTER," SAYS THE LORD. "THOUGH YOUR SINS ARE LIKE SCARLET, THEY SHALL BE AS WHITE AS SNOW; THOUGH THEY ARE RED AS CRIMSON; THEY SHALL BE LIKE WOOL.

No matter how hard a person may try, some issues are just too difficult to manage without appropriate professional help. And while taking advantage of such social services can have enormous benefits, because of the stigma attached to them, many do not consider them as viable options. Whether this is due to individuals' choices or society's influence, the absence of proper counseling and the inability to handle crisis can lead to a feeling of hopelessness.

Regrettably, this is a dilemma that many of us find ourselves in when we don't have the resolve and patience to cope with life's stressful moments. While some persons may be able to recoup from adversity with little or no effort, others find doing so a daunting and emotionally draining task. Instead of making the gut-wrenching decision to reach out for counseling, they sometimes cower in the darkness of despair, unrelentingly clinging to the same destructive behaviors that prevented them from seeking out the resources that could get them back on their feet. But let's not be unsympathetic: no one (including us) wants to admit that they have challenges that they can't handle.

Avid readers of the Bible will tell you that it says, "Man that is born of a woman is of few days and full of trouble" (Job 14). So, no matter a person's social or economic status, all of us at some time in our lives have been or will be discombobulated by life-changing events. And while some may claim to be impervious to such calamities, misfortunes such as sudden illnesses, deaths, and financial changes have been known to send persons to the brink of insanity. Sadly, when people are unable to handle a crisis on their own, self-denial becomes the next best option. So why counseling, and when is it most needed? Hosea 4:6 emphasizes this when it states, "My people are destroyed from lack of knowledge." When a person is no longer able to manage their challenges, it is time to seek godly counsel. As mentioned earlier, in some extreme cases, certified professional help may also be required.

This type of interaction helps persons find not only the tools to cope with life's challenges but also the will to overcome them. The patriarch Job gave us an example of what that really means when his spouse and his friends accused him and attacked his faith (Job 2:9; Job 1:21). Despite his personal suffering, the death of his children, the loss of his livestock, and the destruction of his property, his trust in God's sovereignty kept him strong. For all that he had lost, he regained twice as much (Job 42:10).

Men Women Marriage

42 Days to Victorious Living

WEEK IV: CHALLENGES

STORMS AND MARRIAGE

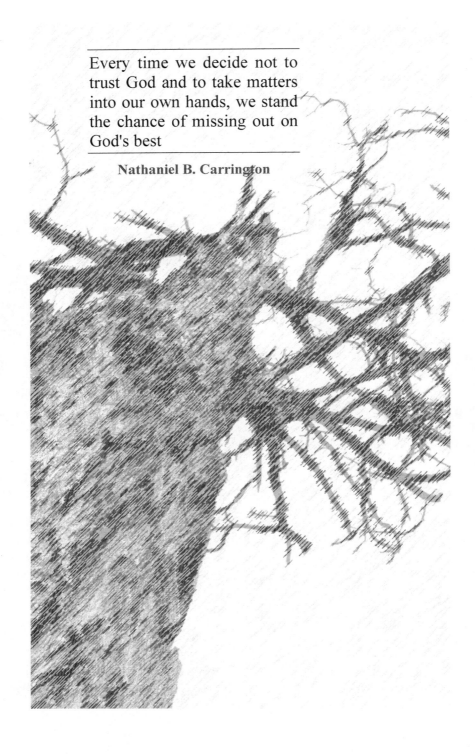

> Every time we decide not to trust God and to take matters into our own hands, we stand the chance of missing out on God's best
>
> **Nathaniel B. Carrington**

Nathaniel B. Carrington

Day 22: FEAR

2 Timothy 1:7 (NIV)

FOR THE SPIRIT GOD GAVE US DOES NOT MAKE US TIMID, BUT GIVES US POWER, LOVE AND SELF-DISCIPLINE.

I wonder what Sarah was thinking as she left the familiarity of her homeland to follow God's calling on her husband's life (Genesis 12). What fears could she have had as she shared with her close friends and family her husband's godly ambitions? If we were there, I think we would have heard some of the many responses from them. Are you crazy? Who does your husband think he is? You are married to a fool. What if... I can only imagine how uncertain she may have been leaving all that she knew behind, to follow a man who believed that God had spoken to him. I know, some of us would say, if I were her, I would have boldly confessed my allegiance to my husband. We seem to forget that the statements made by Lot and his wife suggested the same thing. They agreed to follow Abraham, only to leave him later because of squabbles between their herdsmen (Genesis 13:8). Apparently, this did not send a message of confidence to Abraham's servants. In fact, Lot's early departure sent ripples throughout the camp that led his tribesmen to ask who would lead if something happened to Abraham. After all, he was an old man without any children (Genesis 15:3).

So, let's be honest, we might have found ourselves making the same decision if we were faced with the same unpredictable circumstance (Numbers 23:19). Even Sarah at times exhibited doubt, especially when she laughed at the proclamation that she would have a child at her elderly age (Genesis 18:12 - 13). It is easy to fall prey to doubt and fear when you are uncertain about the outcome of a situation. However, because God's promises are impeccable and his will sovereign, we can trust his words (Numbers 23:19). God made Abraham a promise, which he intended to fulfill in his appointed time (Genesis 15:4). This was very difficult for him and Sarah to understand, seeing that they were past the age of childbearing.

Unfortunately, every time we decide not to trust God and to take matters into our own hands, we stand the chance of missing out on God's best for our lives. Because they gave into their own fears, Abraham, encouraged by his wife, impregnated their Egyptian slave (Genesis 16:3-4). We should not allow fear to drive us to the point of unbelief, especially when the Bible commands that "the just shall live by faith" (Hebrews 10:38). Eventually, Sarah became pregnant with Isaac, as God had promised (Genesis 21:2).

Men Women Marriage

42 Days to Victorious Living

> A healthy marriage is built on a shared vision, with socioeconomic and spiritual benefits trickling down to both partners.
>
> **Nathaniel B. Carrington**

Day 23: SUCCESS

Genesis 39:2 (NIV)

THE LORD WAS WITH JOSEPH SO THAT HE PROSPERED, AND HE LIVED IN THE HOUSE OF HIS EGYPTIAN MASTER.

For some couples, attaining success can be the key to resolving many of the daunting challenges that they face daily. Whether it's a new job or the purchase of a new home, couples usually feel a sense of accomplishment whenever they succeed at doing something together. On the other hand, the success that is purely sought after for selfish reasons can create feelings of insecurity between spouses in any marriage. Like any good business partnership, a healthy marriage is built on a shared vision, with socioeconomic and spiritual benefits trickling down to both partners. If interests, however, become divided because of selfish ambitions, the continuity of the partnership can soon find itself in jeopardy. Regrettably, this may result in one or both partners losing interest and undermining the goals of the business to ensure their own survival.

Sadly, this is the condition of most marriages when one or both spouses feel insecure or alienated because of their partner's ambitions. While most achievements can act as a stimulus that brings couples closer together, many find themselves drifting aimlessly apart. What spouse wouldn't want a beautiful home, a nice car to drive in, or the opportunity to stay at home and raise their young children? Who wouldn't want their husband or wife to live a very successful professional married life?

There is indeed nothing wrong with wanting either of the above. So, what is the real problem with success? Could it be that most of the pushback is mainly because couples often fail to show, or communicate, how these efforts can improve their marriage? The Bible tells us plainly that two are better than one, for if one falls, the other will pick him up (Ecclesiastes 4:9-12).

I personally knew one couple that worked to overcome similar struggles in their marriage. Their misguided views on how advancing their education would impact their marriage created some uneasiness. Fortunately for them, they were able to reassure each other of the long-term mutual benefits that would accompany them if they could achieve these goals. By being open about their concerns, they were able to work together to develop a plan revolving around the demands of their relationship. Instead of falling prey to intimidation or self-centered maneuvering, they made the right decision to handle this challenge together. Thus, both spouses were able to achieve their academic goals with fewer challenges to their relationship.

Men Women Marriage

42 Days to Victorious Living

We should treat our spouse with the presumption of innocence, no matter what suspicions or allegations have been brought against them.

Nathaniel B. Carrington

Nathaniel B. Carrington

Day 24: INNOCENT UNTIL

Mathew 6:14-15 (NIV)

FOR IF YOU FORGIVE OTHER PEOPLE WHEN THEY SIN AGAINST YOU, YOUR HEAVENLY FATHER WILL ALSO FORGIVE YOU. BUT IF YOU DO NOT FORGIVE OTHERS THEIR SINS, YOUR FATHER WILL NOT FORGIVE YOUR SINS.

It always amazes me when a jury makes up their mind on a final verdict without deliberating on the evidence before them. It is as if they don't believe that the phrase "innocent until proven guilty" actually means what it says. No matter the amount of reasoning behind such a decision, deciding on a verdict of innocent or guilty without reviewing relevant evidence sets a dangerous precedent for everyone (Leviticus 19:15). Fortunately, the judicial system has the necessary mechanisms in place to move a trial from a biased environment to a more neutral location. While finding an impartial jury may be much more challenging, the outcome for the innocent party is usually worth the time and effort. Sad to say, some couples handle their suspicions of each other in the same manner.

Instead of upholding accurate and just methods of finding out the truth, they take advantage of the prejudices of their family, friends, and community to justify their own fears and behaviors. They collaborate with persons of questionable motives and character to gain the upper hand in the argument. When this happens, their conversation usually changes from cherishing words to slanderous attacks on each other's character. This is often reflected in their disregard of the possibility that the allegations being made against each other could be untrue.

Regrettably, accusations that are voiced in the presence of individuals with prejudice cannot be easily taken back. In fact, it is sometimes pointless to challenge them, especially after the court of public opinion has made a determination. As a result, even a lie can jeopardize a person's chances of being found innocent (Colossians 3:9).

Knowing this, it should be the goal of every couple to ensure that their marriage is never subjected to this type of fruitless cross-examination.

Such sensitive issues should be addressed in private, with proper counseling. However, if an occasion for reconciliation becomes an insensitive tug-of-war with blame and guilt seated at the table, it is time for both persons to humble themselves and seek each other's forgiveness (Ephesians 4:32). Regardless of the outcome, we should treat our spouse with the presumption of innocence, no matter what suspicions or allegations have been brought against them. This is even truer when the accusations are initiated by those who are close to the relationships, and already hold a bias against marriage.

Men Women Marriage

42 Days to Victorious Living

Getting older does not mean that you suddenly lack the tools to navigate through life's challenges.

Nathaniel B. Carrington

Day 25: AGE

Isaiah 46:4 (NIV)

EVEN TO YOUR OLD AGE
AND GRAY HAIRS I AM HE,
I AM HE WHO WILL SUSTAIN
YOU I HAVE MADE YOU AND I WILL CARRY
YOU; I WILL SUSTAIN YOU AND
I WILL RESCUE YOU.

Most of us spend so much time preparing for the future that we hardly ever get the chance to enjoy the journey. Under such conditions, life can become an ongoing spiral, where the only thing that never changes is change itself. Old age can sneak up on any one of us without warning, bringing to light the fact that we are not as young as we used to be. For most of us, this could be the start of not being able to recognize ourselves in the mirror or a debilitating disease that could inhibit our ability to perform regular day-to-day activities. It is unfortunate that these are some of the only scenarios that most couples associate with aging. Every one of us, starting from the day we were born, has experienced some level of physical or physiological change as a result of growing old. Have you ever noticed how some older children act out whenever there is a life-changing event, such as applying for college or the death of a parent?

The impulsive and sporadic behavior that is sometimes exhibited is usually no different from that of a middle-aged person. In such cases, younger people are said to be acting like teenagers, and middle-aged persons are supposed to be experiencing a midlife crisis. The realization that the future is less predictable as a person gets older can be quite stressful. This could be the reason for some of the erratic behavior that is displayed by some older couples. Purchasing an expensive vehicle, or leaving a loving and devoted spouse of thirty years for a young fling, are just some of the many examples. Such unpredictable behaviors can create havoc in a marriage. Nevertheless, the deliberate action of one spouse to reassure their partner of their continual love and appreciation during such periods is critical. With little to no help, couples who love each other dearly can bring their relationship back to some level of normalcy by making the necessary adjustment.

The fact that an individual is getting older does not mean that they suddenly lack the tools to navigate through life's challenges. David said in Psalms 37:25, "I have been young, and now am old yet I have not seen the righteous forsaken, nor his seed begging bread." Older couples, like teenagers, have a lot to offer to their families and communities. They have the privilege to testify to others of God's faithfulness, especially to those who need the reassurance of knowing that God cares. We should not forget the critical role that Naomi played in her daughter-in-law's life (Ruth 1:3).

Men Women Marriage

42 Days to Victorious Living

When you dispose of what you have to run after a shadow, you are risking the chance of losing what is real

Nathaniel B. Carrington

Nathaniel B. Carrington

Day 26: COMPARING

1 Corinthians 10:12 (NIV)

WE DO NOT DARE TO CLASSIFY OR COMPARE OURSELVES WITH SOME WHO COMMEND THEMSELVES. WHEN THEY MEASURE THEMSELVES BY THEMSELVES AND COMPARE THEMSELVES WITH THEMSELVES, THEY ARE NOT WISE.

While comparisons can be the stimulus that motivates us to strive for greater things, changing the way we look, the things we do, or even the clothes we wear to resemble someone else hardly ever brings satisfaction. Yet we keep trying to find happiness by going after the things by which we measure ourselves. The old Aesop's Fable "The Dog and the Shadow" emphasizes these very points. In this story, a dog was crossing a river with a bone in his mouth. As he began to cross, he saw a reflection of himself in the water, which he thought was another dog with a bone. Not satisfied with his own bone, he grabbed at the one in the reflection. As he opened his mouth, the actual bone fell out, dropped into the water, and was never seen again.

While this is just a simple story, it bears a strong resemblance to the way in which many of us treat our own possessions. This includes the ones that we claim to love so dearly. Whether it is a job, a car, a house, or even a spouse, we never stop to value or appreciate them for what or who they are. Instead, it would seem that we are always willing and ready to trade them in for the latest model. When you dispose of what you have to run after a shadow, you are risking the chance of losing what is real: your marriage, family, friends, and most of all, your self-respect.

It reminds me of the biblical story of Lot, who, because of the problems he was experiencing with his uncle, left the land that they both were living on for a piece that was much more fertile (Genesis 13:8-10). What is so striking about this story is that literally speaking, "the grass was actually greener on the other side." We often fall prey to the misconception that because something is better, it justifies our decision to replace what we have with it. Unfortunately, what started off as a good decision for Lot and his wife eventually became a devastating choice for his entire family (Genesis 19). The belief that changing oneself or one's environment guarantees happiness does not always hold true. As mentioned before, what may have worked for one person in the past will not always work in the future. Sometimes being contented with what you already have is far better than being envious over someone else's stuff (Exodus 20:17). There is an old saying that I always heard my mother say, "If it isn't broke don't fix it."

Men Women Marriage
42 Days to Victorious Living

Trying to get by on young love while paying little or no attention to individual differences will only make matters worse.

Nathaniel B. Carrington

Day 27: CONFLICT

Galatians 5:15 (NIV)

IF YOU BITE AND DEVOUR EACH OTHER, WATCH OUT OR YOU WILL BE DESTROYED BY EACH OTHER.

Instead of learning how to resolve conflict in a marriage, some couples spend their entire lives trying to avoid it. They are misled into believing that the absence of disagreements in a relationship is a sure sign that things are okay. Nothing could be further from the truth. While overlooking squabbles has been known to dissolve differences, it has also backfired in situations where persons felt that they were being ignored. Unresolved or unattended conflict, no matter how minor it may seem to be, is similar to molten rocks sitting at the bottom of a volcano. Eventually, as the pressure rises, and conditions worsen, the eruption becomes an unavoidable natural disaster. For while a volcano can be active, dormant, or extinct, it is the second kind that can do the most damage.

The Merriam-Webster Dictionary defines "conflict" as "a strong disagreement between people, groups, etc., that results in often angry arguments, etc." Sadly, many spouses have never been formally trained or seen good examples of people managing or resolving conflict. As a result, they are usually ill-equipped when situations require them to do so. No matter what a person's livelihood may be, learning how to address and manage issues is an integral part of any human interaction.

Even corporations understand that employees utilizing good conflict-resolution skills will maintain a healthy and productive work environment. Knowing when to listen, speak, and empathize are all necessary skills that are just as important for marriage as they are for any workplace. The fact is, the way that a couple handles conflict will ultimately determine the level of unity that they will experience throughout the life of their marriage. Trying to get by on young love while paying little or no attention to individual differences will only make matters worse. Therefore, it would be in the best interest of every couple to learn how to apply such skills when dealing with disagreements. This could be achieved by either one or both spouses attending formal training or counseling activities. In some cases, it might not be a bad idea to become friends with a godly older and experienced husband and wife. The lessons that can be learned from such a relationship could prove quite valuable in times of conflict. With all of our various character strengths and weaknesses, spouses have a much better chance at overcoming marital strife if they see it as a lack of knowledge instead of individual traits (Hosea 4:6).

Men Women Marriage
42 Days to Victorious Living

> Some circumstances are so complicated that not even a lifetime of friends can help you solve them.
>
> **Nathaniel B. Carrington**

Day 28: FRIENDSHIPS

Proverbs 17:17 (NIV)

A FRIEND LOVES AT ALL TIMES, AND A BROTHER IS BORN FOR A TIME OF ADVERSITY.

Friends, what would you do without them? Always promising to be there when you need them; always telling you what you want to hear; always seeming to have the right answers regardless of the situation. The truth is, God, not your friends, is the only one who can meet your real needs and protect you from ruin (Proverbs 18:24). So, no matter how much your friends may genuinely love you, they are still human beings who were born with limitations (Jeremiah 17:5). The fact is, some circumstances are so complicated that not even a lifetime of friends can help you solve them. While this may be the last thing that a person who is heartbroken may want to hear, it may be what is needed to get them off their rear end and started in the right direction. Though a friend may act like they hold the keys to the mysteries of the universe, this does not mean that they have the answers to your problems.

Sympathizing with a person faced with a problem and earnestly committing it to the Lord is sometimes the only thing that a close friend should do (Galatians 6:2). Regrettably, even if they could do more, how would they know if it was the right thing? There are usually only two sides to a story, and friends, like family, are generally partial to the side that represents the ones that they love, regardless of who is right or wrong. So, no matter how well-intentioned they may be, their actions may only serve to make things even more complicated (Proverbs 13:5).

Therefore, it is not surprising that most friends only find out what the real cause of the problem is after they have falsely slandered the wrong person or persons. We (the brokenhearted) should, therefore, be careful that our request for advice is nothing more than, as the Bible puts it, suffering from itching ears syndrome (2 Timothy 4:3).

When all is said and done, failing to be honest about any situation when seeking advice could be very destructive, not only to the persons involved but also to the one giving guidance. No one should condone wrongful behavior towards anyone, even if the individual in question is your dearest friend. You don't want to be the one to make matters worse by giving premature advice to anyone without knowing all the facts.

Friends of couples should neither be ashamed nor afraid to demand honesty from them when either or both spouses seek their advice (James 3:1). A real friend will always hold their friends to the same standard, regardless of the level of their friendship (Timothy 4:3). I guess the only question that remains is, is it okay for a couple, or anyone, to have friends? The answer is yes (Ecclesiastes 4:12). Nevertheless, couples should choose them based on Christ-centered values and not selfish ambitions or corrupted morals (1 Corinthians 15:33). It is highly likely that one day you may need the godly advice and counsel of a friend, so choose them wisely (Proverbs 12:15).

WEEK V: FAILURE

YOU

ARE NOT PERFECT

Frustration is the only thing that is accomplished when a person relentlessly tries to change something that they have no control over.

Nathaniel B. Carrington

Day 29: FRUSTRATION

Luke 18:1 (NIV)

THEN JESUS TOLD HIS DISCIPLES A PARABLE TO SHOW THEM THAT THEY SHOULD ALWAYS PRAY AND NOT GIVE UP.

The Merriam-Webster Dictionary defines "frustration" as a "feeling of anger or annoyance, caused by being unable to do something." Based on the above definition, it should come as no surprise that frustration is the only thing that is accomplished when a person relentlessly tries to change something that they have no control over. In the case of marriage, it could be one spouse trying to change another's annoying behaviors without any success. What makes such situations, so aggravating is the realization that the person with the annoying behaviors may either be oblivious to their actions or see them as inconsequential, and thus believe that there is no need to change their actions. Regardless of the reasons, this response can cause the offended spouse to languish in frustration, which is usually intensified when the emphasis on correcting the behavior is tied to their happiness.

Unfortunately, situations such as this, compounded by others, can eventually take their toll on both parties, and ultimately create an environment where frustration becomes the norm. The refusal of both spouses to consider how their actions are creating havoc in their marriage is a mistake that most couples fail to recognize until it is too late, and the damage is irreparable. The matriarch Sarah became extremely concerned about her son's future because of the way her maidservant Hagar's son was acting towards him (Genesis 21:9). To resolve the problem, Sarah demanded that her husband send Hagar and her son away (Genesis 21:9-13). Abraham, however, seemed to be more concerned about the welfare of his first son, Ishmael, than about the growing tension that existed between Hagar and his wife. His reluctance to address the situation led to Sarah's frustration, which eventually resulted in her hostile behavior towards Hagar, who, in turn, ran away. Unfortunately, when this becomes the principal way of communicating for a couple, even a loving and caring relationship can quickly become an abusive one. It is therefore important to point out that such situations can also provide a couple with the opportunity to reexamine their relationship, and, if necessary, commit to making the changes that will restore and repair it.

In Abraham's case, this was making the decision along with his wife Sarah to send Hagar and her son away. And while this may vary for different couples, the tough decision to change or stop doing something must be agreed upon by not one, but both spouses. Whatever decision is made, remember that always badgering your spouse can only lead to frustration. There is an old saying, "The only person you can change is yourself." Trust God to do the rest (1 Peter 3:4).

Anyone who has been successful at anything will tell you that being relentless at what you do is a vital part of attaining the good things in life.

Nathaniel B. Carrington

Day 30: EXHAUSTION

Matthew 11:28 (NIV)

COME TO ME, ALL YOU
WHO ARE WEARY AND BURDENED,
AND I WILL GIVE YOU REST.

When an individual in any field becomes exhausted, their productivity often suffers. And while it may only be a one-time drop in their performance, it can still have a significant impact on their overall productivity and monthly or yearly compensation. The Bible tells us: "Let us not become weary in doing good, for at the proper time, we will reap a harvest if we do not give up" (Galatians 6:9). While most persons know only too well the clause "we will reap a harvest," they seem to forget that the real revelation of this scriptural verse is "at the proper time." According to this verse, the only thing that assures your reward is that you keep doing good until good happens to you. If you decide to stop at any time because you are exhausted, you might end up losing the reward. As couples, we are encouraged to keep doing well even when we are weary.

If you have been reading this book from the beginning, you will realize that this is the central theme. A good marriage requires that both spouses commit to doing the things that make their relationship work. Anyone who has been successful at anything will tell you that being relentless at what you do is a vital part of attaining the good things in life. That involves enduring the many challenges that arise from sharing one's life, dreams, and aspirations with another person.

The healthy and substantial changes that result from the deliberate choices made by individuals to better themselves are what can lead to a couple enjoying their marriage. However, if couples are exhausted, they will not be able to commit the time and effort needed to make their marriage work. Similar to employees, exhausted couples can sometimes lose their focus or good judgment when it comes to making good decisions. While it is not my intention to make excuses or overlook marital failures, exhausted people tend to have poor judgment. While a spouse may be willing to overlook minor offensives, such as arriving late for a Friday night bowling session, forgetting to put funds in the account to pay the mortgage is a whole other story on another level. In today's digitally connected world, such incidents can have a disastrous effect on both spouses' credit history. So, what do you do when you are exhausted? Scripture tells us to "lay aside every encumbrance and the sin which so easily entangles us, and let us run with endurance ..." (Hebrews 12:1). While this advice is spiritual in nature, it can also be taken practically. Taking time out to get some rest, prioritizing and eliminating unnecessary tasks, and sitting with a counselor to get a more rounded perspective is helpful. At the end of such changes, things may not be as bad as they look.

Men Women Marriage
42 Days to Victorious Living

> As a drunkard is consoled by his bottle of spirits while at the same time enslaved by it, so too are those caught in the addictive claws of pornography.
>
> **Nathaniel B. Carrington**

Day 31: PORNOGRAPHY

Matthew 5:28 (NIV)

BUT I TELL YOU THAT ANYONE WHO LOOKS AT A WOMAN LUSTFULLY HAS ALREADY COMMITTED ADULTERY WITH HER IN HIS HEART.

According to the Oxford English Dictionary, pornography (porn) is "printed or visual material containing the explicit description or display of sexual organs or activity, intended to stimulate sexual excitement." Addiction, according to the same source, is "an unusually great interest in something or a need to do or have something." Therefore, when an individual becomes fixated on pornography, he or she is said to be addicted to porn. Advancements in technology and a heavily porn-saturated superhighway have now made it possible for anyone to view this material from virtually any place and at any time in the world. Moreover, as the number of individuals that view this material grows, so does the number of those addicted to porn. While some of this material is spread through media outlets such as books, magazines, postcards, and photographs, the web and cable television continue to be the leading sources. What is alarming about this is that many who gain access to this material firmly do not believe that they are doing anything improper.

This notion usually stems from the belief that if no physical contact with another person has occurred, no wrong has been done. After all, how can just looking at another person harm anyone? While this may be partially correct, a simple heartfelt conversation with a recovering addict or former porn worker might just be enough to change this perception. Others who are honestly struggling with this issue may find the biblical views on the subject quite enlightening. In fact, on one occasion, Jesus told his followers, "anyone who looks at a woman lustfully has already committed adultery with her in his heart" (Matthew

5:28). Irrespective of the scriptures and the many testimonies of others, some spouses still believe that they can play Russian roulette with pornography without their relationship being impacted. This irresponsible behavior, if not modified, often leads to either one or both spouses becoming obsessed with or addicted to porn. With that said, porn addiction is no different from any other compulsive behavior. Although it is not a drug, the feelings experienced are similar. Therefore, it should not be treated as any less destructive. Each momentary bout of virtual pleasure leaves the user more and more obsessed.

Eventually, prolonged use leads to an inability to distinguish between healthy and unhealthy sexual desires. As a result, some spouses end up preferring the gratification gained from viewing pornography over the sexual advances of their spouses. Because this happens gradually, couples are often caught off guard by what is taking place in their relationship. Women are often the first to realize that something is not right. This does not mean that men are not just as observant. It also does not mean that women do not fall victim to pornography. However, men are often the ones to display a nonchalant attitude about pornography and its threats to their marriage. Some have attributed this to the different ways in which a man and woman respond to visual and verbal stimulation. The words uttered by Adam when he saw his wife Eve would seem to suggest that he was extremely captivated by her appearance (Genesis 2:23). While it may be unusual to draw such a significant conclusion from just one glance, Adam is not alone in his excitement.

Outside of substantial premarital problems, a groom is often profoundly thrilled by the beauty of his bride as she walks down the aisle towards him. Therefore, it might not be incorrect to conclude that a woman's physical appearance plays a large part in determining how much a man is attracted to her. Those who might be thinking that this refers to physical beauty alone should not forget that "beauty is in the eyes of the beholder" (1 Peter 3:3-4). On the other hand, while the Bible makes no mention of Eve's response to Adam's words, it does share with us her reply to the serpent's questions about God's truthfulness (Genesis 3:1-6; Numbers 23:19; Hebrews 6:18).

The fact that the serpent was able to seduce her into doubting what God said leads to the question: Why didn't the crafty serpent's words have the same effect on Adam? Was he not also in the garden with Eve? Didn't the serpent have the same opportunity to converse with him and cause him to doubt what God said? While the Bible does not explicitly outline the events in the garden, how Adam and Eve acted does prove unequivocally that men and women are different. The Apostle Paul was so convinced of these differences that he emphasized understanding a wife's needs as key to building a healthy marriage (1 Peter 3:7). Therefore, it should not come as any great surprise to either a husband or a wife if their spouse continually seeks clarification of the things they do or say.

For example, many ladies often ask the questions: Why isn't my husband more romantic? Why doesn't he talk to me more about how I feel? Why doesn't he use words to convey his desires to me? While some men often whispered: Why does my wife wait until we are about to have sex to suggest that I don't love her? What does forgetting to call her before I leave work have to do with how much I care? Why do I need to say and do all these things just have sex? After all, aren't we married? As harsh and insensitive as these words may sound, many of us who have been married for some while can concur that at times this has been the state of our relationship.

Unfortunately, couples who experience a lack of intimacy in their marriage often make the fatal mistake of not addressing these innate differences. Instead of trying to educate themselves or seek education about their different needs, they often become sexually detached, leaving each other vulnerable to temptation (1 Corinthians 7:5). God created sex as a form of pleasure to be experienced by men and women in a safe and secure institution called marriage (Hebrews 13:4). In spite of this fact, some spouses prefer a sexual relationship that does not require their sexuality to be open to scrutiny. Pornography, because of its anonymous and non-judgmental environment, offers such individuals the ability to achieve sexual gratification without intimacy.

This virtual world, with its technological accessories, often results in one or both spouses losing the natural desire for each other. When this occurs, individuals are usually either unable or unwilling to let their spouse in for fear of them seeing their inadequacies. Whether this decision to conceal their struggle is due to some deep-rooted psychological problem or to secret shame, if the communication does not return to normal things will continue to spiral out of control.

While this may be nerve-racking for some, the willingness of both spouses to be truthful about their struggles can breathe new life into a relationship. Engaging in healthy communication can create a roadmap that can help couples identify why they are unable to enjoy each other sexually. On the other hand, ignoring a spouse's decision to seek sexual satisfaction outside of their marriage can send them the wrong message that what they are doing is okay. The reality is, couples are more willing to open the doors of grace and forgiveness when they understand each other's struggles (1 Corinthians 13:4-8).

While there is much more that could be written on this subject, because of its immensity, it will have to be covered in a future publication. Instead, we will examine some biblical advice for persons caught in the grip of pornography. We should be conscious of the fact that many of the people in the Bible who overcome sexual temptations are those who either avoid the occurrence or flee from it. Those, on the other hand, who do not follow this same discipline find themselves falling prey to uncontrollable desires (2 Timothy 2:22; 1 Peter 2:11-12).

Jesus, after comparing looking at a woman lustfully to adultery in Matthew 5:28, says in Matthew 5:30: "And if your right-hand causes you to stumble, cut it off and throw it away. It is better for you to lose one part of your body than for your whole body to go to hell." It is clear in this text that Jesus was encouraging his followers to put away those habits or behaviors that caused them to fall into temptation or sin. So yes, there are some practical things that can be done to protect yourself and your family from the influence of pornography. These include restricting access to inappropriate web pages, setting up parental TV controls, sharing social networking and personal email access with a spouse or a trusted family member or friend, and attending intensive workshops that focus on overcoming porn addiction. And last but not least, joining an accountability group to reinforce healthy behaviors that counteract the desire to view porn.

These behavior changes, along with the help of counseling, are just a few of the many things that a couple can do together to protect their relationship from this addiction (Galatians 5:16-24). This holistic approach not only focusses on stopping the compulsive behavior but also restoring the individual's psychological and spiritual well-being. Then and only then will an individual have the best chance of not relapsing into viewing pornography for sexual gratification (3 John 1:2).

> Similar to the covenant between God and man, the marital union requires that both husband and wife be faithful to each other
>
> Nathaniel B. Carrington

Day 32: INFIDELITY

Matthew 5:32 (NIV)

BUT I TELL YOU THAT ANYONE WHO DIVORCES HIS WIFE, EXCEPT FOR SEXUAL IMMORALITY, MAKES HER THE VICTIM OF ADULTERY, AND ANYONE WHO MARRIES A DIVORCED WOMAN COMMITS ADULTERY.

"I heard you in the garden, and I was afraid because I was naked; so, I hid" (Genesis 3:10). The fact that Adam and Eve never considered their nakedness affirms how innocent they were when they were created in the Garden of Eden (Genesis 3:7). It is only after they fell out of a relationship with God that we see them becoming aware of their own nakedness. While their actions did not destroy their relationship, they created an atmosphere of doubt and fear which eventually led to them questioning God's faithfulness. It is disturbing to see how swiftly the consequences of their sin changed the way that they saw each other When Adam was asked, "Who told you that you were naked?" he responded to God by saying, "The woman you put here with me, she gave me some fruit from the tree, and I ate it" (Genesis 3:12).

Before we judge Adam too harshly, a closer examination of the couple's answers reveals that his wife's response wasn't very different. "The serpent deceived me, and I ate" (Genesis 3:13). What was once a beautiful relationship between God and man was now full of distrust, disobedience, shame, and sadness (Genesis 3:17). Sadly, there isn't much difference between what Adam and Eve did and the actions of an unfaithful husband or wife. Similar to the covenant between God and man, the marital union requires that both husband and wife be faithful to each other and their matrimonial vows.

Therefore, having sex with a person other than one's wife is a violation of that union. Unfortunately, instead of considering the emotional pain that infidelity brings on marriage, some spouses choose to focus only on their needs instead of on their marriage. Eve was captivated by what she saw with her eyes, and as a result, she picked the fruit (Genesis 3:6). Whenever we go after something that will endanger the spiritual, physical, and emotional unity of our marriage, we are not wise (Proverbs 6:32). While most marital failures can be addressed and forgiven with time and counseling, infidelity is more challenging. The entanglement of a third party, the possibility of an unwanted pregnancy or the transfer of sexual diseases, and betrayal of marital trust are all consequences of this act.

We should be careful not to believe the lie that "you will not certainly die." Adam and Eve suffered tremendous hurt and pain because of their spiritual infidelity. We should not make the same mistake within our marriage. The Bible tells us that the only way to deal with cheating is to do the same thing that Paul told Timothy (2 Timothy 2:22).

Men Women Marriage
42 Days to Victorious Living

> We should always be careful to examine whether individuals are truly repentant before running off our mouths with a holier-than-thou attitude.
>
> **Nathaniel B. Carrington**

Day 33: FAILURE

Galatians 6:1 (NIV)

BROTHERS AND SISTERS, IF SOMEONE IS CAUGHT IN A SIN, YOU WHO LIVE BY THE SPIRIT SHOULD RESTORE THAT PERSON GENTLY. BUT WATCH YOURSELVES, OR YOU ALSO MAY BE TEMPTED

Who wants to be considered a failure, especially when it comes to something so serious as marriage? No matter which spouse is responsible, both are besieged with the question, whose fault is it? The onslaught of words from both sides sometimes leaves a couple, especially the innocent party, feeling helpless and humiliated. While this behavior may be considered justifiable in certain contexts, it reveals the lengths that some individuals are willing to go to when inquiring about someone else's misdeeds. This ill-advised scrutiny of a couple's indiscretions is usually only successful at doing one thing: adding more confusion to an already delicate situation.

Regardless of who is at fault, no one has the right to ridicule another person. Using the wrongdoings of others to excuse one's own malicious behavior is never the right thing to do (Galatians 6:1). Yes, if the failure is because of one or both spouses' inexcusable actions, then it should be examined (2 Timothy 4: 2). However, if it is not handled correctly, any chance of healing the relationship may be lost in the wind. As the old saying goes, "two wrongs don't make a right." Scripture teaches us that "if anyone is caught in any transgression, you who are spiritual should restore him in a spirit of gentleness" (Galatians 6:1).

We should always be careful to examine whether individuals are genuinely repentant before running off our mouths with a holier-than-thou attitude. Therefore, considering each spouse's behavior, including the circumstances that led up to the unfortunate situation, may be helpful in getting to the root cause of the problem. How we respond should be informed by common sense principles and based on prayer and God's infallible word, not man's ideologies (Colossians 2:8). Also, stupid and irresponsible gossip should be disregarded. On the other hand, partial and impartial information from friends, family, or even the battered spouse or spouses should be scrutinized before accepting it as relevant evidence.

Still, no matter how bad the situation may be, the actions of good-willed individuals, such as a counselor or friends, should not leave the couple feeling abandoned or without hope. Unfortunately, this often happens when hurt couples receive advice from unskilled individuals who need counseling themselves. God and no one else truly knows the condition of a sinner's heart (Jeremiah 17:9). If you are still not convinced about the damage that marital failure can do to a couple, just ask Adam and Eve, the first couple (Genesis 3:12-13).

> Betrayal, whether it is sexually immoral or otherwise, exacts a terrible toll on everyone including the perpetrator.
>
> **Nathaniel B. Carrington**

Day 34: BETRAYAL

SHAKESPEARE'S "TRAGEDY OF JULIUS CAESAR" (ACT I, SCENE II): DESPITE A FOREWARNING, CAESAR IS STABBED IN THE BACK BY HIS FRIEND MARCUS BRUTUS. CAESAR FALLS AND UTTERS HIS FAMOUS LAST WORDS, ET TU, BRUTE? (AND YOU, BRUTUS?).

Of the many hurtful things that one spouse can do to the other, betrayal—no matter how it is done—tops the list. For those persons who studied literature in school, the betrayal of Julius Caesar by Brutus was instrumental in revealing how devastating such treacherous actions are to a loving and trusted friend. Out of all the plays carefully scripted by the well-known poet and playwright Shakespeare, the words *Et tu Brute?* (And you, Brutus?) Uttered by Caesar stand out from them all. Betrayal, according to the online Merriam-Webster Dictionary, is defined as "to deliver to an enemy by treachery or to disclose in violation of confidence." You see, Brutus, out of all the public servants, was held in the highest regard by Caesar. He was the last person that anyone expected would commit such a heinous crime.

In fact, it has been written that "upon seeing Brutus among the conspirators Caesar covered his face with his toga and resigned himself to his fate."[1] This statement would seem to suggest that it was not the bitter sting of his enemies' blades that killed him, but the sight of his friend Brutus with a dagger in hand. Avid readers of Shakespearian literature and documented world history will agree that while the Caesars were no saints, that did not make Brutus's betrayal of Julius Caesar any less grievous than other acts of treason. Not unlike the wounds of Caesar, the Scriptures tell

---

[1] SPOFFORD, AINSWORTH RAND; WEITENKAMPF, FRANK; LAMBERTON, JOHN PORTER. *THE LIBRARY OF HISTORIC CHARACTERS AND FAMOUS EVENTS OF ALL NATIONS AND ALL AGES.* VOL. III. BOSTON: J. B. Millet, 1906. 29.

us that the wounds inflicted by a friend are not only hurtful but also unpredictable (Zechariah 13:6).

The betrayal of Jesus of Nazareth by one of his own disciples, Judas Iscariot, attracted the same type of emotional and painful anguish (Luke 22:4). Those who witnessed the horrific murder considered it to be nothing less than the killing of an innocent lamb (Isaiah 52:14). Judas, like Brutus, plotted with others to kill a person whom they claimed to be their associate and friend.

Although the character and moral purity of Jesus Christ and Julius Caesar are as far apart as day and night, this does not detract from the harsh reality of betrayal. It is no surprise, therefore, that both traitors underwent similar feelings of guilt that eventually resulted in them ending their own lives. Sadly, the same thing can be said about the actions of a spouse who places themselves or their partner in harm's way. Betrayal, whether it is sexually immoral or otherwise, exacts a terrible toll on the perpetrator, as seen in the case of Brutus and Judas. While the person on whom the harm has been inflicted may suffer tremendous pain and even loss of life, the perpetrators are left with the guilt of knowing that they have conspired against their own friend (Matthew 27:4).

> Trying to fix a marriage by hashing out unresolved emotional issues or root causes may only succeed in controlling the fire, not extinguishing it.
>
> **Nathaniel B. Carrington**

Day 35: DIVORCE

1 Corinthians 7:15 (NIV)

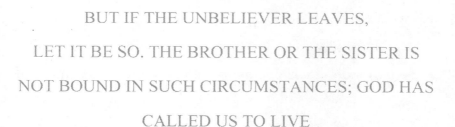

BUT IF THE UNBELIEVER LEAVES, LET IT BE SO. THE BROTHER OR THE SISTER IS NOT BOUND IN SUCH CIRCUMSTANCES; GOD HAS CALLED US TO LIVE IN PEACE.

While many countries have given their citizens the legal and moral right to file for divorce, fornication, and hardness of heart are the only two reasons permitted in the Scriptures (Matthew 19:8-9). During Jesus' period on earth, he explained to the Pharisees that "hardness of heart" was given by Moses and that it was not God's original plan (Matthew 5:31). He also reiterated that divorce and remarriage other than for sexual immorality leads to adultery (Matthew 5:32). Unfortunately, individuals similar to those in our present day were using questionable reasons for divorcing and leaving their wives. Therefore, he found a need to draw a contrast between those unlawful practices and God's commandments. In today's world, where the Bible is no longer seen as the only moral influence, persons may ask what the big deal is.

Many of us fail to see the implications for a society when two individuals decide to get divorced. The number of innocent persons, including children, whose lives are turned upside down because of such a selfish decision, should be cause enough for concern. A healthy marriage does not only contribute to a healthy home, but also to a robust and stable society. Healthy families produce stable children, who usually grow up to be productive individuals within their community. In return, the community is provided with a source of skilled people who can fill the jobs that serve the same community.

While much more can be said about the consequences of having a divorce, it would be wrong to say that marriage does not serve a greater purpose than just making two people happy. We as a community need to help couples seek out other alternatives to divorce. No matter how bad things may seem to be, saving a marriage should still be everyone's priority. Therefore, it is crucial that singles, as well as couples, have a thorough understanding of how to build a healthy marriage before saying "I do" (Ephesians 5:21-33). Trying to fix a marriage by hashing out unresolved emotional issues or root causes may only succeed in controlling the fire, not extinguishing it.

We cannot leave the Creator out of the picture and still expect our marriage to work correctly. Marriage was God's original plan for mankind, and it should be no surprise that he knows how to fix it when things go wrong (Genesis 1:28). Yes, there are some situations where divorce may be the only option. However, before making that final leap, time should be spent with the aid of experienced counselors to examine motives and convictions about what the Bible has to say about divorce.

Men Women Marriage
42 Days to Victorious Living

WEEK VI: GRACE

SEVENTY
TIMES
7

Why forgive? "Without forgiveness life is governed by an endless cycle of bitterness and resentment"

Nathaniel B. Carrington

Day 36: FORGIVENESS

Matthew 6: 14-15 (NIV)

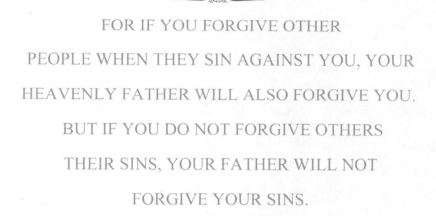

FOR IF YOU FORGIVE OTHER PEOPLE WHEN THEY SIN AGAINST YOU, YOUR HEAVENLY FATHER WILL ALSO FORGIVE YOU. BUT IF YOU DO NOT FORGIVE OTHERS THEIR SINS, YOUR FATHER WILL NOT FORGIVE YOUR SINS.

In one of Jesus' conversations with the Apostle Simon Peter, we hear him talking about the issue of forgiveness. Peter, unlike the other Apostles, was not timid when it came to asking Jesus questions about his earthly purpose. Right or wrong, he always had an opinion on what Jesus was talking about, even if it resulted in him being rebuked (Matthew 16:23). The fact that he was a unlearned fisherman did not stop him from having a substantial dialogue about godly matters (Acts 4:13).

On one occasion, Peter proceeded to ask God how many times he should forgive his brother if he sinned against him. "Jesus saith unto him, I say not unto thee, Until seven times: but, Until seventy times seven" (Mathew 18:22). We are not sure what caused him to ask this question, but we do know that Jesus was speaking about the parable of the unforgiving servant. Some speculate that Peter may have been having one of his customary disagreements with one of the disciples (Galatians 2:11-21).

Nevertheless, in this parable, a certain king had a servant who had a debt which he could not repay. The alternative was to have him and his family sold to repay his debt. Knowing this, the servant fell to his knees and worshiped and begged the king to be patient with him. In response, the king forgave him of his debt because of his passionate plea. Unfortunately, this same servant had a servant in a similar position. And although his servant asked for forgiveness for his debt as he did, he cast him into prison until he could pay his debt. When the king heard of how the servant that he had forgiven treated his own servant, he went back on his former decision and delivered him to the tormentors. The moral is, if you do not forgive, God will not forgive you (Matthew 18:35).

There are things that spouses do to each other within a marriage that can cause them to become unforgiving toward another. Nevertheless, this passage of Scripture lets us know that forgiveness is not only for the individual who caused the harm but also for the one who has been injured. 1 Peter 3:7 tells us that husbands should be thoughtful as to how they live with their wives. I would also encourage ladies to do the same when it comes to how they treat their husbands. Having a healthy understanding of each other's strengths and weaknesses makes giving the gift of forgiveness easier. And finally, why forgive? "Without forgiveness life is governed by an endless cycle of resentment" (Colossians 3:12-13).

Men Women Marriage

42 Days to Victorious Living

> Healthy couples make healthy families, strong families make strong communities, and strong communities lead to economic and social stability.
>
> **Nathaniel B. Carrington**

Day 37: TIMEOUT

1 Corinthians 7:5 (NIV)

DO NOT DEPRIVE EACH OTHER EXCEPT PERHAPS BY MUTUAL CONSENT AND FOR A TIME, SO THAT YOU MAY DEVOTE YOURSELVES TO PRAYER. THEN COME TOGETHER AGAIN SO THAT SATAN WILL NOT TEMPT YOU BECAUSE OF YOUR LACK OF SELF-CONTROL.

No matter the perspective, taking time out to reflect and seek spiritual guidance on issues that impact marriage is not a pointless exercise. While some may consider seeking advice vital to having a healthy marriage, others may view such activities as intrusive schemes created solely to find out personal information. While in some cases this may be true, it does not take away anything from the important role that they play in educating couples. Regardless of the condition of one's marriage, active participation in a recognized marriage-building activity or event can do more to help than hinder. Learning from people who have experienced or are experiencing similar marital challenges can be very enlightening. Couples who have attended such events will tell you that while knowing what works is important, hearing that it actually works can be a very invigorating experience.

The positive energy released during such gatherings not only strengthens the listeners but also gives them the confidence to change. Unfortunately, many people still don't see the value of couples coming together to share information on what works and what does not. What is surprising is that corporate America seems to have gotten this principle right. If the CEO of one of the world's top Fortune 500 companies were to cancel their annual organizational meeting, stakeholders would go ballistic not knowing anything about the condition of their investments (Luke 16:8). As challenging as this may be, spouses need to view their marriages as lifelong investments with enormous returns. We need to accept that we are the stakeholders of our marriages and that their condition hinges on how we manage them. Therefore, the continuity of marriage as an institution should not be seen as any less significant than that of a corporation. While each tends to differ regarding how they pursue their goals, they are both socially and economically intertwined.

Healthy couples make healthy families, healthy families build healthy communities, and healthy communities lead to economic and social stability. Couples that set aside time to improve their marriages benefit not only themselves but also their communities. While there may be many reasons for not attending a marriage-building activity, when you consider other options, you may begin to see things differently (Proverbs 11:14 KJV).

Men Women Marriage

42 Days to Victorious Living

> Whatever advantages could be gained from seclusion, is often lost due to the absence of a strong social support structure.
>
> — Nathaniel B. Carrington

Day 38: ISOLATION

Genesis 3: 8-10 (NIV)

THEN THE MAN AND HIS WIFE HEARD THE SOUND OF THE LORD GOD AS HE WAS WALKING IN THE GARDEN IN THE COOL OF THE DAY, AND THEY HID FROM THE LORD GOD AMONG THE TREES OF THE GARDEN. BUT THE LORD GOD CALLED TO THE MAN, "WHERE ARE YOU?" HE ANSWERED, "I HEARD YOU IN THE GARDEN, AND I WAS AFRAID BECAUSE I WAS NAKED; SO I HID."

The Merriam-Webster Dictionary defines "isolation" as "the state of being in a place or situation that is separate from others." While this is not the aim of most, resisting the urge to isolate oneself from the difficulties we face is a lifelong struggle. The anxieties and fears brought on by life problems is not only real but also unnerving. While some are successful at working through their challenges, others often become detached and immobilized by them. Instead of accepting the assistance of others, they retreat into their secluded bunkers, hoping that these issues would somehow disappear or resolve themselves. Unfortunately, if conditions worsen or become more evident to others, then the only thing that is achieved by these actions is further isolation.

This does little to stop the conundrum of problems that usually surrounds such situations. Therefore, whatever advantages could be gained from seclusion, is often lost due to the absence of a stable social support structure. No other story in the Bible illustrates this better than that of Abraham and his nephew Lot (2 Peter 2:7). His decision on two separate occasions to separate from his uncle proved consequential for his life and his family. Despite his uncle's continual plea for him to return, Lot's was resolved to go his way. His rejection of the offer eventually resulted in the death of his wife's, an incestuous affair with his two daughters, and the isolation of his generation from their kinsmen (Genesis 19:1-36).

If nothing else is learned from this story, separation, especially during stressful times, can have an adverse impact on one's ability to make sound decisions. The truth is no matter how independent we may believe that we are, we should not be surprised when someone reminds us that no one is self-sufficient. As my mother always told me "no man is an island" and "It takes a village to raise a child." Lot's story is a fitting example of what you should not do when facing challenges.

We should never be too eager to separate ourselves from the people that we are connected to, especially those who know us best. While you may not immediately find the answers, you may hear something that might point you in the right direction (1 Corinthians 12: 16, Ephesians 4:11-13). How do you know if God hasn't placed the answer to your dilemma in their hands (Galatians 6:2)?

When all is said and done, failing to be honest about any situation when seeking advice could be very destructive, not only to the persons involved but also to the one giving guidance.

Nathaniel B. Carrington

Day 39: HONESTY

1 Titus 2:7-8 (NIV)

IN EVERYTHING SET THEM AN EXAMPLE BY DOING WHAT IS GOOD. IN YOUR TEACHING SHOW INTEGRITY, SERIOUSNESS AND SOUNDNESS OF SPEECH THAT CANNOT BE CONDEMNED, SO THAT THOSE WHO OPPOSE YOU MAY BE ASHAMED BECAUSE THEY HAVE NOTHING BAD TO SAY ABOUT US.

Why do I need to be honest with people? For as long as I can remember, I have never been honest with anyone. So why should I be honest with my spouse? Even if I wanted to, I wouldn't know where to start or what to do. Unfortunately, this is the reality that far too many couples find themselves faced with when living with a mate who lacks the character or integrity to be truthful. Nevertheless, before we decide to judge a person's actions, it may be important to first identify the root cause of their behaviors.

Most psychotherapists believe that most of the behaviors that emerge during the teen years are usually learned during one's early childhood and adolescence. The period from birth to eight years and older, including the human interactions, play a significant role in shaping our beliefs about lying or telling the truth. For most of us, this involved the manner in which our birth family or legal guardian exemplified such behaviors when we were growing up.

Therefore, close attention should be given to how parents and caretakers respond to children whenever they are caught in a direct lie or refuse to tell the truth. Teaching them practical ways of resolving situations without lying will not only help them to be honest but also be good communicators. Still, while behavioral reinforcement techniques can encourage the development of good character traits, it is a child's natural inclination to lie when faced with the consequences of telling the truth. Children who find themselves struggling with habitual dishonesty as they get older are prone to continue doing it throughout their adult lives unless interventions occur. However, while there are some extenuating circumstances and social anxiety disorders that can cause this phobia, lying to avoid telling the truth is still the primary stimulus.

Regardless of the rationale, such behaviors can create unwanted feelings of insecurity and paranoia, which can cause an angry spouse to act in an unseemly manner. While such responses have been known to work in some relationships, they have also backfired, doing more harm than good, in others. Since it seems that it is little that anyone can do to ensure that a spouse is actually telling the truth, both partners should see that it is in the best interest of their marriage, to be honest with each other (Hebrews 10:24).

Men Women Marriage

42 Days to Victorious Living

Repentance, therefore, involves much more than being sorry for the wrong done to another person.

Nathaniel B. Carrington

Day 40: REPENTANCE

Luke 17:3 (NIV)

"IF YOUR BROTHER OR SISTER SINS AGAINST YOU, REBUKE THEM; AND IF THEY REPENT, FORGIVE THEM."

No one can ever prove that I did anything wrong. It is already done and over with. How is repenting going to change anything? How is it going to help anyone, least of all me? All of us, at some point in time, have found ourselves using similar arguments to justify not repenting for wrongs that we have done. Instead of trying to understand how our lives and those of others were impacted, our focus was placed mostly on keeping our pride and image intact. The old saying "let sleeping dogs lie" seems to be more relevant during such times than amending one's behavior (Proverbs 18:15). Some may argue that reflecting on the past is an unproductive use of one's time and energy. However, those who are familiar with the story of the prodigal son know that it may be the only thing that could halt a person's life from spiraling into a deadly pattern of destructive behaviors.

This story tells us about a young man who, after wasting his entire inheritance living an immoral lifestyle, found himself alone and destitute. The parable ends with the son repenting of his actions and returning to his loving father, who was patiently waiting for him to come home. The Merriam-Webster Online Dictionary defines repentance as "to turn from sin and dedicate oneself to the amendment of one's life."

Repentance, therefore, involves much more than being sorry for the wrong done to another person. In fact, a quick analysis of the life of the prodigal son reveals that repentance usually has more to do with the spiritual wellbeing of the offender and less to do with the offended. It was only after the son had genuinely repented that he saw the actual impact of his selfish ambitions on his family and friends. While there was money in his hand, he didn't consider the pain that he was inflicting on the heart of his father. Neither did he stop to think about the feelings of those around him, especially his brother, whom he had left in the field (Luke 15:17-21; 15:25-28). The fact that he was unable to see how his actions were destroying his own life reveals the real dangers of living with unforgiven sin (James 1:22; Luke 15:14-16).

The money, friends, and wayward lifestyle did not give him the fulfillment that he thought it would. Instead, the only thing that it did was to rob him of his peace and innocence (John 10:10), the same qualities that he once cherished when he submitted to his thoughtful and loving father. Unfortunately, some spouses find themselves in the same sinful position, and thus, they forfeit any opportunity of having a loving marital relationship. In Luke 5:31-32, "Jesus answered them, 'It is not the healthy who need a doctor, but the sick. I have not come to call the righteous, but sinners to repentance.'"

Too many individuals go into marriage focusing on the physical love while paying little attention to the sacrificial love that marriage requires from us.

Nathaniel B. Carrington

Day 41: LOVE

1 Corinthians 13:4-8 (NIV)

LOVE IS PATIENT, LOVE IS KIND. IT DOES NOT ENVY, IT DOES NOT BOAST, IT IS NOT PROUD. IT DOES NOT DISHONOR OTHERS, IT IS NOT SELF-SEEKING, IT IS NOT EASILY ANGERED, IT KEEPS NO RECORD OF WRONGS. LOVE DOES NOT DELIGHT IN EVIL BUT REJOICES WITH THE TRUTH. IT ALWAYS PROTECTS, ALWAYS TRUSTS, ALWAYS HOPES, ALWAYS PERSEVERES. LOVE NEVER FAILS. BUT WHERE THERE ARE PROPHECIES, THEY WILL CEASE; WHERE THERE ARE TONGUES, THEY WILL BE STILLED; WHERE THERE IS KNOWLEDGE, IT WILL PASS AWAY.

Everyone, from the cradle to the grave, has experienced love in one capacity or another. And while it is manifested in so many ways around the world, God's love is expressed by the voluntary death of Jesus Christ on the cross. We get a glimpse of how much God loves us when the Scriptures say, "For God showed his love to us that while we were yet sinners Christ died for us" (Romans 5:8), And in another passage of Scripture, where it states, "For God so loved the world that he gave his one and only Son, that whoever believes in him shall not perish but have eternal life" (John 3:16).

Unlike the love that is so often portrayed by secular media, God sets a standard for us that can only be experienced when we exhibit it within our own earthly marriage (Ephesians 5:25-33). It is then that we realize that it is much more than a feeling or a physical exercise in intimacy. Such love demands from us a commitment to our mate that is like that of a soldier in the army. It is not solely the erotic love that is so often portrayed on the many billboards, paintings, song lyrics, movie scripts, and book publications. These are all expressions of love that many accept without questioning their origin.

Too many individuals go into marriage focusing on the physical love while paying little attention to the sacrificial love that marriage requires from us. The result is devastating for many young couples, who soon discover that it takes more than just physical intimacy to build a healthy marriage. Of the many kinds of love recorded in the Greek language, *agape* love, which involves compassion, forgiveness, and charity, stands out above all the rest. And while the others, such as *eros* and *phileo*, include many similar values, *agape* exhibits behavior that is capable of loving at a level that is next to God. This unselfish love that holds the one being loved in high regard is indeed fitting for a husband and wife. "Love is patient, love is kind. It does not envy, it does not boast, it is not proud. It is not rude, it is not self-seeking, it is not easily angered, it keeps no record of wrongs. Love does not delight in evil but rejoices with the truth. It always protects, always trusts, always hopes, always perseveres. Love never fails" (1 Corinthians 13:4-8).

Men Women Marriage

42 Days to Victorious Living

> Navigating through marital life without prayer isn't much different from sailing a boat in the middle of the sea without a compass.
>
> Nathaniel R. Carrington

Day 42: PRAYER

Luke 18:1(NIV)

THEN JESUS TOLD HIS DISCIPLES A PARABLE TO SHOW THEM THAT THEY SHOULD ALWAYS PRAY AND NOT GIVE UP.

1 PETER 3:7 (NIV)

HUSBANDS, IN THE SAME WAY BE CONSIDERATE AS YOU LIVE WITH YOUR WIVES, AND TREAT THEM WITH RESPECT AS THE WEAKER PARTNER AND AS HEIRS WITH YOU OF THE GRACIOUS GIFT OF LIFE, SO THAT NOTHING WILL HINDER YOUR PRAYERS.

I

If you are familiar with family dynamics or have read the material covered in this book, you may have realized by now that some challenges cannot be solved without the intervention of prayer. From as far back as I can remember, the saying "the family that prays together stays together" was used to describe a way of life that couples were taught to practice to have a dynamic and unwavering relationship. Although my birth family and religious upbringing were centered solely around this adage, it wasn't until I became a husband and father that I was able to fully appreciate its true meaning.

Like newlyweds, a captain and his crew are usually very confident when setting out to sail in their new and shiny vessel. However, if there is no compass on board to guide them to their destination, then the journey can be disastrous. This is particularly the case if icebergs are in the area. Navigating through marital life without prayer isn't much different from sailing a boat in the middle of the sea without a compass. Even adopting ideologies like the ones found in this book can end up destroying a marriage if used insensitively and incorrectly by one or both spouses.

Unfortunately, arriving at this understanding can be quite daunting for persons who rely solely on themselves to overcome life's obstacles. No matter how many books you may have read on this subject, there is always that one curveball that can slowly sneak up on you and hit you, WHAM! Moments like these in life reinforce the fact that there are some situations that you cannot handle on your own. Sadly, such occasions can leave a person feeling overwhelmed and shaken to the very core of their being. Nevertheless, it is usually at this juncture that the power of prayer becomes self-evident, as individuals are unable to resolve their own challenges.

During this period, it is not surprising to see wealth and status rapidly give way to the desire to pray (Matthew 6:9-13). This intangible resource that did not seem available before eventually begins to take back its rightful position, removing self-defeating attitudes and replacing them with hope and faith, and helping couples to accomplish the very things that they know they could not do with their own strength alone. This causes them to see the grim reality ahead not as a time of calamity, but as an opportunity for God to reveal himself in their lives.

Regardless of ethnicity, race, or culture, we can always take comfort in the Scripture that says, "men ought always to pray and not faint" (Luke 18:1). We will all have dark days, some more than others. Nevertheless, we are encouraged by Scripture: "Do not be anxious about anything, but in every situation, by prayer and petition, with thanksgiving, present your requests to God" (Philippians 4:6). "And the peace of God, which transcends all understanding, will guard your hearts and your minds in Christ Jesus" (Philippians 4:6-7).

Men Women Marriage

42 Days to Victorious Living

ADDITIONAL READING

WORDS MATTER

If you keep telling a spouse, child, or anyone in your sphere of influence that their lives will never amount to anything, don't be surprised when they don't.

Nathaniel B. Carrington

Nathaniel B. Carrington

SELF-FULFILLING PROPHECY

Proverbs 18:21 (NIV)

THE TONGUE HAS THE
POWER OF LIFE AND DEATH,
AND THOSE WHO LOVE IT
WILL EAT ITS FRUIT.

The fact is, of all the marital challenges that I find troubling, a self-fulfilling prophecy is the only one that continues to mystify me. While there are other problems much more grievous and easier to identify, this one, because of the way in which it evolves, can go undetected for years before being noticed. Whether this is due to a lack of understanding or the unpopularity of the term is another subject. In any case, couples, regardless of their position or status in life, continue to fall prey to its deadly grip. And unfortunately, the longer it takes to identify and address this issue, the greater the damage that is done to the couple's relationship.

What is a self-fulfilling prophecy, and how do you know when the challenges that you are facing are a result of one? The truth is, short of evaluating every single behavior that may have contributed to a problem, there is no way of telling. This is why being able to recognize the causes and actions that have contributed to a problem is crucial to identifying when you have one.

The Cambridge Advanced Learner's Dictionary & Thesaurus defines "self-fulfilling prophecy" as "something that you cause to happen by saying and expecting that it will happen." In other words, speaking or having an expectation about a person or thing such as a husband, wife, child, or marriage can affect one's behavior towards that subject, and ultimately cause it to respond accordingly. With that said, the first thing that any couple or counselor should ask is, how much of the problem is as a result of the couple's own words or expectations and how much is not?

Using a quick analysis, if the majority is the former, then it is likely that the marriage is experiencing the effects of a self-fulfilling prophecy. Unfortunately, most individuals lack the necessary skills to make such a diagnosis. Therefore, it is critical that they seek the right mixture of spiritual and professional help before assigning responsibility to either spouse. While the term self-fulfilling prophecy speaks for itself, trying to separate self-inflicted wounds from those caused by third parties can be an unending process, one that if done incorrectly could make matters worse.

While many may still not agree with the above, we should not forget that the type of person that our children become is usually mainly a result of our words and expectations. And while it is true that some apples do drop far from the tree, those that meet our expectations substantiate the belief that words and expectations can actually shape the lives of people. Therefore, we can conclude that successful adults (husbands and wives) are the product of their own or someone else's positive words and expectations. Regrettably, when this occurs, the term "self-fulfilling prophecy" is usually excluded from descriptions of the situation. The fact is, many believe that the term "self-fulfilling prophecy" should only be used when the outcome is unfavorable to the subject.

As preachers, we know only too well the power of the spoken word and the effects that it can have on a person's life. In one of the more popular passages of Scripture, Jesus compares the spoken word to the seed used by a farmer to grow crops. He carefully explains to his disciples that in the same manner as a seed goes into the earth and brings forth fruit, so can a word be placed in the heart of a man or woman.

So whether in private or public, yesterday or today, one or five years ago, your words and expectations are destined to shape the lives of someone (Matthew 13:23). Considering this fact, we should be more careful with the words that come out of our mouths (Matthew 4:4). If you keep telling a spouse, child, or anyone in your sphere of influence that their lives will never amount to anything, don't be surprised when they don't. If this is your situation or that of someone in your life, then you may be witnessing a self-fulfilling prophecy right before your eyes (Proverbs 18:21).

TESTIMONIALS

TESTIMONIAL I

I am a visual learner, and I like it when I cannot only hear what is being said but can have a visual to go along with it. The perspective clips with the pictures and the points of accepting one another's different perspectives brought such clarity to a problem that is so prevalent in marriages today. I know it helped us. Thank you, for your dedication to God and your marriage. Your transparency with your own lives helped us, and I know others that were there also. Many blessings to you and your husband.

TESTIMONIAL II

I was very much appreciative of the focus of this conference – helping couples and singles obtain a better understanding of what is required to be a loving couple.

TESTIMONIAL III

The message was clear, and the PowerPoint enhanced the message. I loved the perceptions' pictures. The topic on covenant is so essential because so many people don't focus on the agreement. The audience participation was effective. The audience asked questions and stated what they learned...yeah! The break with snacks was a good idea. The time/location was convenient.

TESTIMONIAL IV

The part that blessed me the most was the subject of Perceptions. I wish my husband was there. Now I understand that it's ok for us to see things differently. We have to now come together with our different views and make it work for our marriage. Thanks for being such a blessing!!!!

TESTIMONIAL V

My husband and I have been married for some time now, and it's the first conference where he is attentive. Though he's in a different place spiritually, the conference gave us practical tools to apply at home. We've heard and seen it all but nothing sticking to the ribs. I would like to say thank you for being obedient to the Spirit of God; for waiting when he said to wait and moving when he said move. Had it been a different time, we would have missed this moment. Blessings to you and your family.

TESTIMONIAL VI

This a very much needed ministry for singles and couples, very spiritual.

TESTIMONIAL VII

Both my husband and I enjoyed Ministering by skit, and we would not hesitate to do it again if you ever asked or needed us to. I'm just grateful that I was able to help in getting the word out to as many folks as possible because I know so many people who could benefit from such a Blessed, informative and empowering conference. In the future, please don't hesitate to ask for my/our assistance if needed and as always, we will be more than honored, privileged and blessed to help in any way we can. Both my husband and I are looking forward to part 2 and so is everyone else from our ministry who attended. I will make sure your thanks and acknowledgment letter to our ministry and Pastor and Minister is read during the announcement time on Sunday. Until next time, may God continue to bless, prosper and grow this ministry like never. Keep up the good work!

TESTIMONIAL VIII

This ministry provided foundational principles for us to build and establish a stable marriage. Often our counseling sessions were utilized to exemplify respect, honor, and compromise within our daily marital life. Pastor Nathaniel emphasized following essential Bible scripture: 1 Corinthians 10:13, "and now these three things remain, faith, hope, and love but the greatest of these is love." Thank you, Pastors Nathaniel and Carolyn Carrington for your valued time and teachings that have made our marriage stronger and pleasing to God.

DAILY QUOTES

by Nathaniel B. Carrington

WORDS

MATTERS

43 DAILY QUOTES

DAY 1. QUOTE

If you want to know someone better, asking them a question is still the best approach.

DAY 2. QUOTE

Woman was made to be man's equal and not his subordinate, to rule with him and not be ruled by him.

DAY 3. QUOTE

Having the support of a loving and healthy family environment is key to developing good relationship skills.

DAY 4. QUOTE

Love, and not money, should be the only reason why two people should walk down the aisle to spend the rest of their lives together.

43 DAILY QUOTES

DAY 5. QUOTE

We should never be duped into believing that the only way to true happiness is to "Keep up with Mr. and Mrs. Jones

DAY 6. QUOTE

Regardless of what people may think about work and the roles of men and women, money, not gender, is the only commodity that the bank will accept.

DAY 7. QUOTE

Retrospection is usually best for separating infatuation from facts when making life-changing decisions.

DAY 8. QUOTE

Smile, it is not your similarities or matching garments that matters.

DAY 9. QUOTE

Inconsiderate behavior in any form can lead to uneasy feelings in any marriage

---

DAY 10. QUOTE

Ultimately, the Scriptures never intended for submission to be used as a means of controlling others, especially our spouses.

DAY 11. QUOTE

We should never assume that we know what service means to our spouse. Instead, we should ask them, and maybe, if we are lucky enough, they might just tell us

---

DAY 12. QUOTE

Outside of the challenges associated with marital failures, such as infidelity, addictions, and other dubious behaviors, sex should be satisfying.

43 DAILY QUOTES

DAY 13. QUOTE

The Scriptures remind husbands that leadership is modeling obedience to Christ's word within your own marriage.

DAY 14. QUOTE

Decisions, no matter the intentions, have consequences. Assessing the pros and cons before making them is always the wisest thing to do.

DAY 15. QUOTE

Marriage is much more than just meeting expectations.

DAY 16. QUOTE

Doing nothing while crying over one's predicament does little to help anyone

Nathaniel B. Carrington

DAY 17. QUOTE

Children are usually not emotionally ready to understand or cope with adult problems

DAY 18. QUOTE

If "an apple a day" can keep the doctor away, then I am confident that "a dinner a day with your spouse" will keep the divorce lawyer at bay.

DAY 19. QUOTE

Godly dressing starts with the word modesty.

DAY 20. QUOTE

The malicious use of words can have devastating effects, not only on the originator but also on the listener and the person being slandered

DAY 21. QUOTE

When a person is no longer able to manage their challenges, it is time to seek godly counsel.

DAY 22. QUOTE

Every time we decide not to trust God and to take matters into our own hands, we stand the chance of missing out on God's best

DAY 23. QUOTE

A healthy marriage is built on a shared vision, with socioeconomic and spiritual benefits trickling down to both partners.

DAY 24. QUOTE

We should treat our spouse with the presumption of innocence, no matter what suspicions or allegations have been brought against them.

DAY 25. QUOTE

Getting older does not mean that you suddenly lack the tools to navigate through life's challenges.

DAY 26. QUOTE

When you dispose of what you have to run after a shadow, you are risking the chance of losing what is real

DAY 27. QUOTE

Trying to get by on young love while paying little or no attention to individual differences will only make matters worse.

DAY 28. QUOTE

Some circumstances are so complicated that not even a lifetime of friends can help you solve them.

DAY 29. QUOTE

Frustration is the only thing that is accomplished when a person relentlessly tries to change something that they have no control over.

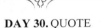

DAY 30. QUOTE

Anyone who has been successful at anything will tell you that being relentless at what you do is a vital part of attaining the good things in life.

DAY 31. QUOTE

As a drunkard is consoled by his bottle of spirits while at the same time enslaved by it, so too are those caught in the addictive claws of pornography.

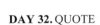

DAY 32. QUOTE

Similar to the covenant between God and man, the marital union requires that both husband and wife be faithful to each other

43 DAILY QUOTES

DAY 33. QUOTE

We should always be careful to examine whether individuals are truly repentant before running off our mouths with a holier-than-thou attitude.

DAY 34. QUOTE

Betrayal, whether it is sexually immoral or otherwise, exacts a terrible toll on everyone including the perpetrator.

DAY 35. QUOTE

Trying to fix a marriage by hashing out unresolved emotional issues or root causes may only succeed in controlling the fire, not extinguishing it.

DAY 36. QUOTE

Why forgive? "Without forgiveness life is governed by an endless cycle of bitterness and resentment"

DAY 37. QUOTE

Healthy couples make healthy families, strong families make strong communities, and strong communities lead to economic and social stability.

DAY 38. QUOTE

Whatever advantages could be gained from seclusion, is often lost due to the absence of a strong social support structure.

DAY 39. QUOTE

When all is said and done, failing to be honest about any situation when seeking advice could be very destructive, not only to the persons involved but also to the one giving guidance.

DAY 40. QUOTE

Repentance, therefore, involves much more than being sorry for the wrong done to another person.

DAY 41. QUOTE

Too many individuals go into marriage focusing on the physical love while paying little attention to the sacrificial love that marriage requires from us.

DAY 42. QUOTE

Navigating through marital life without prayer isn't much different from sailing a boat in the middle of the sea without a compass.

43 DAILY QUOTES

DAY 43. QUOTE

If you keep telling a spouse, child, or anyone in your sphere of influence that their lives will never amount to anything, don't be surprised when they don't.

DEVOTION NOTES

DEVOTION NOTES

DEVOTION NOTES

DEVOTION NOTES

DEVOTION NOTES

ABOUT THE AUTHOR

ABOUT THE AUTHOR

PASTOR CARRINGTON

Pastor Nathaniel B. Carrington is an author, international Bible teacher, conference speaker, and biblical counselor with a passion for helping people overcome relationship challenges. His engaging and illustrative style of teaching helps him transcend both cultural and denominational barriers. The central theme of his teaching focuses on assisting individuals to develop excellent listening and communication skills. He believes that being an effective communicator is crucial to having a successful life.

Pastor Carrington is the co-founder and president of Revealing Word Ministries (rWm), a nonprofit organization located in Boston, Massachusetts. This organization hosts a number of exciting conferences throughout the year. Participants come away from each event with a knowledge of how practicing good interpersonal communication skills can improve relationships within the home, church, and workplace. He is a frequent guest on local radio programs and is currently working on his own television program,

ABOUT THE AUTHOR

CommuniCate Now, for local cable television. He is the author of the book, The I-IV-V Approach to Composing Songs, and the founder of Carriconec, an organization that focuses on helping couples, singles, and youth learn healthy life skills. This involves personalized training in music, information technology, and business ethics.

Pastor Carrington has inspired many of his peers through his unique and practical teaching style to strive to be the best at whatever they do. His ability to listen and interpret both verbal and non-verbal communication as well as empathize with others has helped him to become a more efficient Biblical counselor. He has earned both B.S. and M.S. degrees from Northeastern University, along with some other certifications from the University of Maryland, the University of Virginia, the University of New Mexico, and Berklee College.

Pastor Carrington and his wife, Carolyn, a talented leader in her own right, work well together as they endeavor to teach others the benefits of effective communication, in both small and large groups, throughout the United States, the Caribbean, and the entire world. They are the proud parents of three children, John, Gabriella, and Daniel.